TANTRISM

The secret principles and practices of the
left-hand path of Hinduism.

By the same author

ANGKOR EMPIRE: A Cultural History of the Khmers
BEYOND THE BODY: The Human Double and the Astral
  Plane
ENCYCLOPEDIA OF ESOTERIC MAN
ENCYCLOPEDIA OF METAPHYSICAL MEDICINE
HINDU WORLD: An Encyclopedia of Hinduism (2 vols.)
MASKS OF THE SOUL: The Facts Behind Reincarnation
PERSIAN PAGEANT: A Cultural History of Iran
SEX AND THE SUPERNATURAL

TANTRISM

Its Secret Principles and Practices

by

BENJAMIN WALKER

THE AQUARIAN PRESS
Wellingborough, Northamptonshire

First published 1982

© BENJAMIN WALKER

British Library Cataloguing in Publication Data

Walker, Benjamin
 Tantrism.
 1. Tantrism
 I. Title
 294   BQ8915.4

 ISBN 0-85030-272-2
 ISBN 0-85030-273-0 Pbk

Printed and bound in Great Britain.

CONTENTS

PREFACE

Tantrism in its higher reaches might be regarded as part of the traditional religious complex of the East, and as such is more generally acceptable to the orthodox, its writings being hardly distinguishable from the approved texts of medieval Hindu and Buddhist philosophy.

In this book I am concerned not so much with the acceptable face of Tantrism as with its more unconventional image. This aspect of the religion, Tantrism as popularly understood in India, represents the nether side of the Eastern esoteric tradition, and belongs to a wider cultural stream, whose tributaries ramify over India and many parts of Inner Asia. It is neither Hindu nor Buddhist, but represents a religious undercurrent, with sources anterior to these religions, and flowing through a different level of territory. Its scriptures are treated by believers as having an authority equal, and sometimes superior, to the Vedas and other sacred writings of orthodoxy.

Because of its association with magic and the occult, this 'left-hand' form of Tantrism is rejected by the orthodox as antinomian in principle and abhorrent in practice. Its basic sacramental features are widely divergent from those that form part of the usual Eastern pattern of worship. The attitude of Tantrism to social conventions, its dedication to the female principle, and its emphasis on sexuality, make it one of the most extraordinary of all beliefs, and unique among all other religious systems of the world.

The full story of the evolution and spread of Tantrism still awaits its historian. With so much secrecy, so much hostility and persecution, and such a large-scale destruction of its scriptures, it is inevitable that much remains obscure. Conflicting assertions by different authorities cannot always be reconciled by verification from original sources, many of which are now lost. I have therefore confined myself to noting the broad flow of the movement, both outside and within the Indian subcontinent.

The great figures of the Tantrik past are all but forgotton in the land of their birth. The towering personage of Padmasambhava, who taught in India and Tibet, does not figure in the history of Indian Buddhism. Bodhidharma, founder of the Dhyana sect is likewise unknown in India. Many other famous teachers, including Shenrab, Bogar, Kanipa, Matsyendra and Gorakhnath, can at best be accorded only semi-legendary status. As matters stand today it is impossible to disentangle the historical from the fabulous in the biographical material about them available to us.

The chapter on Tantra in the West could have been expanded into a separate book, to embrace the whole area marking the influence of Eastern cult teachings on the work of European and American writers, musicians, artists and thinkers. Here too, I confined myself to the broadest outlines.

Eastern occultism in its many strange forms exercises a terrible fascination over certain people, and those not armed with healthy scepticism and common caution often succumb to its lure. The final chapter reflects the views of many observers, Eastern and Western, experts in their field, who have devoted their lives to the subject, and their warnings are well worth serious consideration.

The Bibliography covers many major English works on Tantrism, as well as books and articles relevant to related matters treated here. I am deeply indebted to my brother Alexander Walker who kept me provided with a constant supply of books and magazines from India that were of the greatest help to me in my work.

Note: I have avoided the use of diacritical marks for Sanskrit words, and have adopted spellings commonly used in popular works on the subject.

B.W.
Teddington

1.

THE PRINCIPLES

Tantrism comprises the beliefs and practices of an Eastern cult of great antiquity, which in various forms and with local variations is known in India, Bhutan, Sikkim, Nepal, Tibet, Manchuria, China and other contiguous regions.

The writings in which its doctrines are enshrined are known as the Tantras, a name of obscure origin, and variously said to be derived from Sanskrit root words signifying: 'body', because of its emphasis on bodily activities; 'stretch', because it extends the faculties of man; 'rope', because it secures the devotee to his deity; 'harp', for the music and beauty of its philosophy; 'interiorness', for the secrecy of its doctrines.

Most commonly the word tantra is said to come from the Sanskrit word meaning 'loom', suggestive of the two cosmic principles, male and female, that make up the warp and woof of the woven fabric of the universe.

The emphasis in Tantrism is on the female. The spinning of thread, like baking, plaiting and basketwork, was an essentially 'distaff' or feminine occupation, and the spinster, or one who did the spinning, was always a woman.

Also linked with the idea of the weaving female are the spinning deities, who are responsible for the fate or destiny of men, such as we find in the mythologies of the Greeks, Norsemen, Slavs, Chinese and other early peoples. The whole universe is said to be woven by the gods, and invisible cords hold the cosmos together.

As the universe is held in a web, so the life of the individual hangs by a thread. In ancient Indian writings God is compared to a spider 'who envelopes the universe in threads', and there is a reference to the cosmic 'thread-breath' (sutratma), twining strands that keep the universe spinning until the end of time, when the cords will break and the universe fall apart.

Although some tantrik authorities decline to call Tantrism a religion or a philosophy, and speak of it as practice, it possesses all the features that constitute a religion, including its own deities, its own priesthood and theology, its own principles and ways of thought.

Its underlying philosophy is as complex as any that can be found in the major religious systems of India, China and Tibet. Indeed some of it reaches heights of metaphysical subtlety to match anything that can be found in the traditional theologies, and is indistinguishable from them.

But at another level some of its precepts and practices are diametrically opposed to these systems, and the more conservative deplore its unorthodoxy, its occultism, and its sexual emphasis, which they find religiously unacceptable and morally repugnant. These latter features are made up of a mixture of primitive magic, the tribal lore of ancient shamanist Asia, and age-old fertility rites.

Shiva and Shakti
In tantrik cosmology the whole universe is seen as being built up, pervaded and sustained by two basic forces which are in intimate and intricate union. These forces, named Shiva and Shakti, are personified as male and female deities; Shiva representing the constituent elements, and Shakti the dynamic potency that causes these elements to function.

Shiva is also a god of destruction, and he has many strange and sinister attributes, as we can deduce from the titles accorded him. He is Mahakala, meaning Great Black One, and also Great Time, that is, the dissolver and slayer of all things temporal. He is also the Terrible; the Lord of Demons; the Wrathful; the Mad; the Black Limbed; the Great Ascetic; the Red One; the Nude; the One with the Phallus Erect; the Phallus Holder; the Lord of the Coital Act; the One with Golden Semen.

Shiva's consort is Shakti, the female principle. Her name means 'power', for she represents the primal energy underlying the cosmos. She too has many forms, some benign, such as Parvati, goddess of beauty; some tragic, like the goddess Sati; and some terror-inspiring, like Kali.

The tragic destiny of Sati began when her husband Shiva was

insulted by a celebrated sage *(rishi)* during a feast. Humiliated by the affront to her husband, Sati threw herself into the sacrificial fire. This legend forms the basis of the terrible Hindu rite of *suttee*, now proscribed but still occasionally practised in the rural districts of India, in which a widow burns herself on the funeral pyre of her husband. The disconsolate Shiva recovered the partially burnt corpse of his young wife and bore it away with him. As he did so fragments of her limbs and organs fell to earth in 108 different sites *(pithas)*, each site to become in time a renowned place of pilgrimage. The big toe of the goddess fell near Calcutta, and her organs of generation in Kamakhya, Assam.

One of the terror aspects of Shakti is personified in the goddess Kali. The word *kali* means 'black', as well as being the feminine form of *kala*, 'time', and is equated by the German scholar Hermann Güntert with a Greek word meaning both 'time' and also the process of attaching together the threads on a loom, suggesting once again the association of this goddess with weaving, time and destiny.

Kali is the dread goddess who brings in her train pestilence, famine, war and violence. Her favourite animals are jackals, ravens and vultures. The notorious band of murderers in northern India known as the thugs used to throttle their victims in her honour. In the past, human sacrifices were offered at her temple near Calcutta, but today she is propitiated with the blood of goats. One of her lesser titles is Dhumavati, 'the Smoky One', after the fumes arising from the freshly slaughtered bodies of her sacrificial victims.

Kali is often shown dancing on corpses, and is portrayed black of visage, wearing a garland of human skulls around her neck. In her two right hands she holds a bloodstained sword and a dagger; in her two other hands are severed heads dripping blood. Blood dribbles down her chin, her long tongue lolling out of her mouth. In a terrible image representing her as 'the One with the Severed Head' (Chhina-masta), a headless Kali holds her own decapitated head, while her mouth greedily drinks the blood spurting from her neck. This fearsome goddess is honoured as Jagan-matri, 'Mother of the World'.

Kali Yuga

The name Kali, and related words like *kali* and *kala*, are derived from the Sanskrit root *kal*, signifying to 'drive' or 'impel', and implying a hurrying towards a predetermined end. According to the medieval Indian writings known as the Puranas, four great ages or *yugas* demarcate the destiny of mankind, and the name Kali is given to the last of these four ages. Each of the yugas is shorter than the one preceding it, and each is characterized by the progressive spiritual, moral, mental and physical degeneration of the human race.

The first age was one of truth and righteousness, its colour was white, its metal gold. At that time there was only one complete and unified religion, and only one Veda or sacred book, susceptible of one interpretation only. The second age was characterized by knowledge, its colour was red, and its metal silver. The Veda now had four interpretations. The chief feature of the third age was ritualism, its colour was yellow, its metal copper, and there were four Vedas.

These three ages have already elapsed, and we are now well into the final stages of the fourth and final age, called the Kali yuga, characterized by lawlessness. The colour of this yuga is black, and its metal lead. The Kali yuga is marked by the absence of righteousness. True worship has ceased, the outward trappings of religion are confused with piety; and greed, hatred, duplicity and strife prevail. It is a time when property and wealth confer rank, and money is the mark of virtue. Spiritual, mental and physical diseases are rampant. Everywhere there are signs of moral degeneration and spiritual decay.

There is an excessive preoccupation with things material, sensual and monetary. Cooks are given coronets, and dancing girls are held in higher esteem than women of virtue. No value is placed on the marriage vow, on social contracts, personal obligations and duties. Servants become arrogant, seeking to emulate their masters. Youth no longer obeys its elders, and the elders no longer merit obedience. Husbands and wives no longer respect each other, because they are no longer worthy of respect.

Men resort to other men's wives and to virgins, who in turn have no compunction about accepting their embraces. Men and women seek satisfaction outside the marriage bond, delighting in intercourse with persons of their own sex, and even with animals. Men become emasculated and feeble, and women rise to positions of importance, taking over the responsibilities of the male.

In this yuga the four Vedas are fragmented and corrupted, and subject to countless confusing and contradictory interpretations. These once-sacred texts are now powerless, like serpents divested of venom, like barren women who can bear no issue, like sterile trees that can give no fruit, like wall-paintings that cannot move, like puppets that move without understanding.

According to Tantrism, the Vedas, while appropriate to the earlier epochs, are clearly quite irrelevant to the present age. For this reason, and to meet the needs of mankind in its current predicament, a new set of doctrines is required. Material desires must be met. Physical appetites must be appeased. Sexual urges must be satisfied. Man's aspirations in all these directions must be ritualized, and physical passion and sexual gratification elevated and transformed into an act of worship.

The scriptures in which these principles are promulgated and the practices in which they are set forth are the Tantras, which are held up by tantriks as the true and indeed the only scriptures of the Kali yuga.

The Texts

There are scores of Tantras, Hindu and Buddhist, written in various languages, but they all have a characteristic flavour. The treatises are sometimes presented in the form of a dialogue between the god Shiva and his consort Shakti, in the course of which the general teachings are expounded, and the practices to be followed are described.

Taken collectively, they deal with such matters as: the creation of the world, along with an elaborate cosmology; the three great ages through which the world has passed, concentrating in particular on a detailed account of the fourth and present Kali age; the names of the different gods and goddesses, with their status and powers; the forms of worship appropriate to each deity; miscellaneous ceremonials for acquiring magical powers; the dissolution of the world.

The Tantras also give instruction on the various modes of divination by astrology, horoscopy or other means; on esoteric physiology, with emphasis on the plexuses *(chakras)*; mental and spiritual discipline; breath control and physical culture, especially as prescribed by hatha yoga; the art of internal alchemy; the construction of magical designs *(mandalas)*; the intoning of words of power *(mantras)*; and the acquisition of magical power *(siddhi)* for the control of others and of the forces of nature.

Some of the teachings deal almost exclusively with erotics, and are largely variants of the sexological treatises for which India is famous. There are long passages on such matters as the art of erotic enjoyment; forms and methods of intercourse; the art of erection, retention, repetition; ritual copulation. Great emphasis is laid on sex magic and sex mysticism.

Tantrism appears to have originated in some region outside the north-west borders of India, and first came to India as an oral tradition. In about the eighth century the teachings began to appear in written form, among them the *Guhya-samaja Tantra*, one of the oldest texts, followed in the next century by the *Hevajra Tantra* and others. These early manuals were written by Buddhists, with Hindu Tantras following in the ensuing centuries. The *Kularnava Tantra* belongs to the twelfth century, and the greatest of all the Tantras, the *Mahanirvana Tantra* probably dates from the eighteenth century.

The style of the texts varies considerably. The early Buddhist treatises are undoubtedly the work of learned scribes but some of the later ones are written in what has been described as 'religious pidgin' and 'barbaric Sanskrit', and distinguished by 'an abominable style', the material often being little more than a plagiarized rehash of earlier works.

In India Tantrism seems to have developed along reactionary lines, motivated perhaps by those who could not suffer the tyranny of the brahminical priesthood or tolerate Buddhist austerity. The writings do not express a philosophy that is calculated to endear them to the orthodox. The texts are therefore not regarded as canonical, and are not mentioned among the fourteen branches of literature recommended in the Hindu lawbooks.

From time to time tantrik writings were destroyed by Hindu and Buddhist zealots because they clashed with the orthodox teachings. Of those that remained many were later burned by the Muslim invaders who found the doctrines reprehensible and anti-religious, and guilty of openly advocating idolatrous practices. All this created the need for greater secrecy, with the result that much of their teaching was communicated orally and never put down in writing.

Because of this systematic destruction of the Indian Tantras, the major part of the extant tantrik texts is found outside India in non-Indian languages, so that only the translated and often mutilated and edited versions survive. The actual number of tantrik writings in existence is not known. In one listing of Indian works 64 texts are named, in another 84, in a third 108. Besides, there are literally thousands of later Tantras and commentries on the Tantras, some consisting of a few pages and some considerably bulkier.

If we include certain texts of Taoism and the Tibetan canon, much of which is of a tantrik nature, we find the number of extant writings expand enormously. The Taoist canon, the *Tao Tsang*, consists of 1200 volumes, vast portions of which deal with tantrik teachings on breath control, internal alchemy and sex mysticism.

The Tibetan Buddhist canon consists of two massive collections, the *Kanjur*, comprising 108 printed volumes, and the commentaries on them, called the *Tanjur*, consisting of 225 volumes, together totalling over 4500 texts. Of this material a great deal is devoted to Tantrism, including a description of the mystic circle of the gods and goddesses paired off; collections of spells for calling down the deities; rites of sexual union; and various ritual devices that are purely tantrik.

Even excluding the Tibetan canon and the secondary material published in Japanese and Chinese, a complete tantrik bibliography, according to Agehananda Bharati, would make a book of about 700 pages (1965, p.303).

Secrecy

Tantriks advocate the most stringent concealment of their beliefs and practices, and Tantrism virtually forms a kind of secret society whose mysteries are closely guarded from the outside world. The *Kula-chudamani Tantra* states that the principles, which originate from the god Shiva, are not to be divulged to the uninitiated, not even to the gods Brahma and Vishnu.

Certain teachings are therefore always communicated orally,

the master whispering them direct into the disciple's ear. There is a long history of such 'ear doctrines' *(karna tantra)*. These are of an extremely recondite nature, and are never set down in writing, being transmitted by the master to selected pupils after long preparation and many arduous trials.

Some Tantras contain so-called 'sleeping texts', which are not 'awakened', or explained, except for the purpose of communicating some part of them to students of prime qualification. Such teachings as are embodied in written form are frequently draped in a series of almost impenetrable veils of symbolism, themselves requiring special instructions to unravel.

Others are expressed in what is called a 'twilight language' *(sandhya bhasha)*, ostensibly meaning one thing, while actually signifying something quite different. This was achieved either by employing a peculiar gnomic language of extreme brevity, or by extensive recourse to figurative speech designed to mystify the uninitiated, and thus effectively putting the texts beyond the comprehension of anyone who did not possess the code for their decipherment.

In any event, all such texts, even when disguised, were carefully secreted. In Tibet, where Tantrism was widely taught and practiced, certain magical texts were kept under lock and key.

Esoteric elements of the teachings were also embodied in sculptured representations, paintings and other works of art, including architecture. Many features of the tantrik temple, from the outer courtyard through the pillared porch to the little dark cell in the interior containing the deity and his consort, enshrined tantrik principles in symbolical form.

Secrecy was also maintained during times of persecution by burying the more arcane cult writings. The legend of such interred texts, although not unknown in India, is especially widespread in Tibet, where they are known as *ter-ma*, 'buried treasure'.

In Tibetan tradition it is said that Srong-tsan-gam-po (d. A.D. 698), the first Buddhist king of Tibet, placed a number of Bon (pre-Buddhist), Buddhist and tantrik texts in metal caskets and had them interred in various parts of the country. Even more prone to hide his teachings in this way was the great tantrik teacher Padma-sambhava (fl. A.D. 750) who did so both because he felt that the time was not ripe for the doctrines to be disclosed, and because in his view none of his disciples was fitted to receive and perpetuate them.

Rumours of such buried scriptures naturally led to the search for them, and in the course of centuries several of these texts were allegedly brought to light. The fortunate ones who recovered these treasures, usually following some dream or revelation, formed an exclusive sect, the *Rong-lugs*, named after the first of the treasure hunters (Rao, 1977, p.73). The poor quality of most of these discovered masterpieces, however, of which large collections exist, leaves little room for doubt that many were faked compilations of dubious antiquity and little cultic merit.

Even today Tantricks lay considerable emphasis on the secret perpetuation of their system. They declare that other teachings, which are expounded promiscuously for all to see and understand, are like common harlots who expose their persons and give their favours to all. Tantra, on the other hand, is like the chaste and virtuous wife, who reveals her beauty and bestows her gifts only to her lawful husband.

Secrecy, they say, lends coherence and strength to their doctrine, which weakens when its merits are exposed. It enhances the beauty of the system, and makes what it offers all the more desirable. If non-tantriks became acquainted with their teachings, without due understanding, they might be tempted to follow them and despoil them of their worth and virtue.

Tantriks claim to be a community of the elect. They have evolved a code of cryptic finger signs *(chhoma)* by which they can recognize others of their class. They have their own philosophy, and their own form of worship offered to their own deities in their own way. The rites take place at night, at venues known only to the elect.

Ritualism

In Tantrik philosophy, knowledge is valueless, true happiness impossible, good deeds fruitless, and power a vain pursuit, unless attended by appropriate ritual *(sadhana)*. This ritualistic side of Tantrism was developed to the full in all forms of worship *(puja)*, and is evident in particular in the preparatory rites of purification and dedication, in the initiation of a new pupil, in the installation and worship of an idol, in meditation, and above all in such practices as the worship of the vulva and the phallus, and other rites of a sexual nature.

Invisible energy is believed to be drawn down during the ceremonies, imbuing the chief hierophant and his assistants with the necessary power, which they in turn transfer to objects and participants by the rite of 'applying' (nyasa). In this, the priest ritually places his hand upon some person or object to communicate power by touch. It has countless variations. Thus, the priest might place his hand on an idol, to draw out some of its power, and then lay his hand upon the tantrik aspirant and so ritually transfer the power to that person. Or, a worshipper may place the fingertips of his right hand on a stone phallus, and then touch his own phallus, in order to charge it with phallic energy. The first object need not actually be touched, but in that case the touching must be powerfully visualized.

The more complex rituals are accompanied by all the elements familiar to Western exponents of sorcery, and are reminiscent of the rites of high magic prescribed in the Western grimoires. The working tools, the implements and utensils, the accoutrements of those taking part, all have a basic similarity to the Western forms: the wand (danda), the chalice (patra), the musical instruments, the incense, and the water and oil for anointing and sprinkling. Like their Western counterparts, the participants of a tantrik ritual wear the proper vestments, the ceremonial neckwear, the girdle, the ear-rings (a feature of some tantrik sects), and the protective amulet (kavacha).

In Tantrism we find the same preoccupation with ceremonial paraphernalia, the same concern for auspicious times and days, the construction of the right kind of temporary altar, correctly oriented, and the exact disposition of all the participants in the appropriate quarters; and there is the same emphasis on occult gestures (mudras), and magic circles (mandalas), all accompanied by words of power (mantras).

Mandalas
The mandala is a magical diagram, commonly circular in outline, which is treated as a special sacrosanct area where various high-powered operations take place. Ceremonial rites

accompany the making of such ritual patterns, which may be traced on the ground, or painted on paper, fabric or animal skin, engraved on bone, wood or metal, and sometimes marked on the body.

Mandalas need not be visibly drawn, or objectively delineated. Adepts of high degree can create their own mandalas mentally, while others are the result of the personal introspection of past masters meditating on the 'planes'. The designs of such undrawn or indrawn mandalas are never made known, except to those to whom they are communicated telepathically.

The mandala always represents a three-dimensional figure, even though it is drawn flat. The Bon sorcerers of Tibet dance out the mandala, hopping this way and that as they trace the required pattern with their movements. Mandalas may also be raised architecturally. The ground-plan of Eastern temples will often be seen to bear a striking resemblance to the mandala. In itself the design of the mandala may be even more than three dimensional, for its extensions are believed to reach out into the planes of the astral world and the abode of the gods and demons.

As stated, the outline of the mandala is usually circular, but it may occasionally be drawn in some other symmetrical shape, like a square, triangle, pentagon, or with a stellar, radiating, crystalline or floral design, 'concentred' about a fixed point. In any case, a circumscribing circle is always regarded as present, even if invisible. It may be oriented in a specific direction as required by circumstances.

Within the outline of the mandala are drawn various lesser squares, circles and triangles, which demarcate the whole into a number of zones, dedicated as sanctuaries for the different deities. Sometimes the figures of the deities and their spouses, along with their weapons, emblems and secret signs, and temples, altars, palaces, parks and fountains are painted in, in rich colours, forming a complex tableau of occult art. Every detail of the design is steeped in symbolism, transforming the mandala into a temenos or sacred zone, an archetype of holy ground.

In the sorcerous left-hand rites, the zones of the mandalas are dedicated to the lords of the nether regions, and the paintings differ correspondingly. There may be graveyard scenes, dancing skeletons, drawings of demons armed with dagger and spear in attitudes of menace, and their obscene female companions, along with representations, actual or symbolic, of the sexual organs.

By means of meditation, and the recitation of mantras and magical invocations, the spirit entities, good or evil, deities from the heavenly spheres, demons from the infernal regions, are summoned to occupy the places allotted to them, and the mandala becomes instinct with their presence.

Essentially, the mandala is treated as a focus of occult force, and is used both to attract and empower the energies of the other spheres. It provides a place for the spirit entities, and at the same time emanates potent radiations like a talisman. It then becomes a *yantra*, an 'engine' of power, a psychological and spiritual 'apparatus'. Such mandalas are regarded as having a life of their own.

A well-known mandala of this kind, called the *shri-yantra* or 'glorious yantra', is based on the triangle motif, being sexual in character and purpose. In the centre is a dot, symbolizing the seed or semen. This is contained within a downward pointing triangle, representing the vulva, which itself is contained within an upward pointing triangle, representing the phallus, and these again within downward and upward pointing triangles, making a series of interwoven triangles, commonly nine in number, representing the active interplay of vulva and phallus in coition, the whole design being surrounded by rings and lotus petals. The outer border of the shri-yantra, as of all mandalas, acts as a protective barrier against the intrusion of unwanted powers and alien influences, and also helps to confine and concentrate the powers engendered within the enclosure.

All the parts of a mandala are interconnected, and every point and line has a meaning. There are believed to be direct correspondences between the various quarterings of the mandala and the occult planes. It is, in effect, the static form of a dynamic process, and is given vitality by the forces of the unseen world.

The mandala is regarded as an *axis mundi*, a crosspoint of the world, whose geometry is believed to be linked with the greater geometry of the cosmos, providing, as it were, a map of the universe, and in this sense is spoken of as a cosmogram. It is also regarded as a psychocosmogram, a diagram of the interior workings of the mind of the cosmos, or a plan of the cosmic consciousness.

Less pretentiously, it is treated as a psychogram, or a plan giving access to the secret pathways leading into the labyrinth of the human mind. Different mandalas are used for different purposes. Meditation on one kind of mandala can convert it into a powerful focus of psychic energy, and it may then be used as a 'healing picture'. Another may reveal what is within, involving one in confrontation with the hidden self. Yet another may trigger a mental reflex, precipitating an out-of-body experience, and cause one to take a 'trip' into the astral planes, with their gates and thresholds and terrifying guardians who block the path unless the correct password is given.

The images that appear before the mind's eye during meditation on a mandala, whether beneficent or terrifying, are said to be reflections of the interior consciousness. According to a Hindu text, these figures 'are images of thy own mind, contributions of thy own thought'. Psychologists of the Jungian school regard the mandala in its many variations as symbolizing the structure of the deep psyche.

The mandala has a universal diffusion. In varying guises it is found represented in the art and architecture of almost every culture in the world. The circle and the sphere, and their countless associated symbolizations, all share the same idea. Also part of the mandala mystery is the notion of squaring the circle. In different contexts the mandala is said to represent the sun, the disk, the ring, the ouroboros (the serpent with its tail in its mouth), the female breast, the vulva, the clock face, the ball, the round table, the eye.

In Western occultism the analogue of the mandala is the magic circle, but here the practitioner stays within the circle so that the powers invoked remain outside, prevented from entering the circle by the protective circumference. In the East the invoked powers stay within, the practitioner remains outside.

The mandala epitomizes the quintessence of form: it is related to form as the mantra or magical vibration is related to sound. It might best be described as the visible and tangible embodiment of the mantra, and indeed it is often treated as a kind of soundless mantra with its own impulses radiating outwards.

Mantra

The mantra is a sound, syllable, word or brief verse that is believed to have a special potency. In the Eastern occult view, sound *(shabda)* includes both the 'struck sound', caused by air vibrations, such as the sounds we ordinarily experience, as well as 'unstruck sounds', that is, the silent sounds heard internally. In Hinduism the science of these mystical phonemes is known as *mantra-yoga* or *shabda-yoga*.

Since the mantra is regarded as a nucleus of power and a form of energy, its enunciation is said to set up pulsations that energize both mind and body and, what is more, can carry enlightenment. Great importance is attached to the study and practice of these mystical sonances, and exponents dwell at length on the relationship between tonality *(svara)* and illumination *(svar)*.

Magical phonemes are not uniquely of Indian origin. They are known to almost every ancient civilization. The word mantra itself is derived from an old Iranian root-word meaning 'to think', implying an interior process. The intrinsic power of the intoned sound was known in China, Mongolia and Central Asia from early times and belongs to the earliest strata of Tibetan belief. The name of the pre-Buddhist religion of Tibet, Bon, means, 'to mutter magical spells' (Rao, 1977, p.3). In India the concept of the magic of sound probably originated in the eastern regions. M. N. Dutt states that the custom by which the guru communicates a mantra to his disciple is purely tantrik in origin; it was first introduced into Bengal by Bengali tantriks and afterwards imitated in other parts of India.

The mantra may take many forms. It may be a short verse *(shloka)* from the ancient scriptures; a phrase or word of special significance; the name or title of a deity; a series of syllables strung together; a single syllable or simple sound; the letters of the Sanskrit alphabet, with rhyming variations. Unlimited powers are said to reside in the shorter mantras, especially the mystical monosyllables, or seed-sounds *(bija-mantras)*.

The most famous mantra, commonly rendered *om*, is a magical tri-sonant made up of three letters, A U M, and is thought to hold the key to the universe. Like *om*, many of the other seed-mantras end on a deep humming note, such as *m, n* or *ng*, for example, *hrim, ain* or *sring*. Each of the tantrik deities has his own seed-mantra: *gam* for Ganesh; *krim* for Kali, *krom* for Shiva. Several short exclamations used by Hindus and Buddhists during their religious ceremonies have also passed into the mantra class, such as *vashat*, 'well done', *svaha*, 'hail', and *phat*, 'crack', the latter used by Buddhists as a verbal weapon for driving off obstructing spirits, the fingers being snapped around the head while it is being uttered.

Many mantras are taken direct from the sacred texts, but they may be received in other ways. Some are said to be recovered from the records imprinted in the ether *(akasha)*, where they are believed to be permanently stored. Some may come as an inspiration during a waking vision or in a dream. A mantra may be sent down by the deity to the devotee during worship, prayer or meditation. Some are put together like an anagram and serve as a mnemonic device. A few were composed by poets and mystics, and some were condensed by the rishis or sages of old from larger literary works.

There is a special method of reducing a large work to such a hermetic formula. Thus, a scriptural text of several thousand verses is first summarized in a single chapter. This will again be reduced to a paragraph and then to a line, and finally to a single syllable. So powerful is this final précis that, like a microdot, it will contain the essence of the full treatise, and mastering the mantra, it is believed, will give a man an intuitive understanding of the whole text.

Many mantras are communicated by the guru or teacher whispering the mantra into the ear of the pupil, and such aural communication can reveal the secret doctrines instantly. A story goes that an ignorant workman who was busy near the window of a house where a mantra was being whispered by the master to the pupil, overheard the mantra and in a flash received instant enlightenment and understanding of the entire doctrine, as though it had been taught to him over many years.

Some mantras have no meaning for the uninitiated, and their deeper significance will come even to the initiated only through meditation and repetition. The identical mantra can reveal different meanings to different persons, depending on the grade of their advancement in the understanding of cult doctrine.

It is very important that the mantra be correctly pronounced and intoned. Mantras may be chanted, they may be hummed or whispered, or they may be meditated on in silence. Says the *Kularnava Tantra*, 'Mantras done mentally are the best'. But however done, a mantra is enriched, empowered and activated by repetition *(japa)*. Repeating a mantra causes its deeper mysteries to be understood. Repetition helps to induce a xenophrenic or trance-like state and bring on mystical illumination. When repeated, a mantra penetrates the supernatural planes and in a way coerces the gods or demons to do one's bidding and grant one's request.

Many extraordinary promises are held out to those who successfully carry out such repetitions a prescribed number of times. Thus, the person who repeats a certain mantra one *lakh* (100,000) times will find that all men and women will obey him implicitly. If he repeats it two *lakh* times he will be able to control the elements. If ten *lakh* times, he will be able to travel over the universe.

Special rosaries are sometimes used to keep a tally of the number of times a mantra is repeated. These usually consist of dried seeds on a string, but when sinister powers are sought by the tantrik the smaller bones, or pieces of bone of men and animals are strung together. Human teeth and snake vertebrae can also take the place of seeds. Some texts prescribe different beads for different purposes: crystal beads for petrifying a person; wood for bewitchment; human bone for causing hatred; the bone of a brahmin for conjuring up spirits; the bone of an elephant for rain; the bone of a buffalo for killing.

Certain mantras are believed to be endowed with their own vitality and do not have to be consciously repeated by the tantrik. If correctly uttered they need be chanted aloud only ten or twelve times for them to carry on repeating themselves internally day and night, whether the person is awake or asleep, and without him having to keep up the reiteration himself. A periodical booster might be given once every few hours to keep the mantra reverberating.

Mantras may be written on ritual objects or in the spaces of a mandala diagram. They may be stamped on the body. They may be visualized in their written or symbolic form. They may be identified with worldly objectives, powers and functions, and meditated on to bring them to fruition. A mantra may be concentrated on, then projected outwards in the form of an invocation, command, blessing or curse, to function as a protective shield, a healing potency, or a defensive or destructive missile.

The mantra may be directed internally to a particular part of the body, such as the head, between the eyebrows, the solar plexus or the sex organs, and at these points it can be made to generate vibrations that create strengthening or healing energies. Those directed to the cranium set up resonances in the chambers of the skull, resulting in a kind of heightened awareness. Sometimes a mantra is sent on a journey around the body and its reverberations cause the old bodily tissues to fall away and make place for new and regenerated ones.

It is believed that there exists a mantra for every illness, for every condition, and for every purpose. Any problem, no matter how complex or difficult, can be resolved by intoning or meditating on the appropriate mantra. Mantras can be used to subdue the enemy, sap the strength of rivals, irresistibly attract women, tame fierce animals, bewitch, slay and destroy, cause crops to fail, make cities tremble, and bind the gods to one's will.

There is no limit to the number of mantras that can be formed. Reputedly, there are ninety million seed-mantras alone, and the longer mantras are beyond counting. According to the *Mahanirvana Tantra*, there are an 'endless number of mantras', a million, ten million, a hundred million, a million million. Which mantra is to be used, for what purpose, and in what manner, is best determined by the guru.

The Guru

Central to all forms of initiation and indeed to all tantrik ritualism, is the person of the guru, the spiritual preceptor or cult leader. The mere theoretical knowledge of tantrik teachings, or uttering the words of a mantra, or performing the outward actions of a ritual ceremony, do not convey enlightenment or communicate power. Important truths do not come through the study of books or independent contemplation, but are the result of wisdom received and handed down through an unbroken chain of appointed leaders, of whom the guru is the living representative.

The esoteric truths of Tantrism can therefore only be

transmitted by one who has been divinely endowed to receive
them in the first instance. The secrets of the cult are 'stored' in
the guru, who is the repository of these truths. The guru is the
living flame, and he alone can charge the unlit wick of the pupil
(*chela*), duly dipped in the oil of cultic teachings, with the divine
light. Practical initiation is impossible without a guru.

It is essential that the tantrik aspirant learn what he has to
from a qualified guru. Many meditative techniques are difficult
and even physically and mentally dangerous, requiring expert
and experienced guidance. The same applies to practical
observances and spiritual disciplines, which can only be taught
and supervised by qualified mentors. As M. P. Pandit, a yoga
scholar states, 'The guru enters into the being of the seeker,
implants himself within him and conducts the *sadhana* or
spiritual discipline' (Caycedo, 1966, p.36).

The selection of the right guru thus becomes imperative in
cult practice. Whether the chosen guru will accept a particular
chela is another matter.

The Tantras unequivocally and repeatedly emphasize the
necessity of paying great respect to one's guru. Slandering one's
preceptor is the first of the fourteen basic 'downfalls' for a pupil.
Celebrated gurus in the cultic hierarchy will even be given the
homage due to the deity, and in fact the identification of the
guru with God is part of an ancient Indian tradition.

Initiation

The truths of tantrik doctrine cannot be acquired, and tantrik
practices cannot be effectively performed, unless the chela or
pupil has been duly initiated. The ceremony of initiation
establishes a relationship and sets up a link between chela and
guru, between guru and the spiritual cult chain, and between the
cult chain and the deity.

The period of pupillage may last for many years, when the
theory is taught to the aspiring tantrik. Before the actual
initiation he undergoes a long period of fasting and asceticism,
as well as certain tests of endurance. The actual process of
initiation, known as *diksha*, 'enhallowment', can take place in
many ways, each consisting of several stages.

It starts, as a rule, with a ritual prayer and homage to the guru
by the candidate, after which the candidate's knowledge of

sectarian doctrines and practical teachings is put to the test. When satisfied with this, the guru communicates a mantra, a secret word or phrase, to the pupil. He is given guidance for visualization, which is important if he is to generate and augment his own magical powers.

This is followed by the rite of 'applying' (*nyasa*), when the guru places his hand on various parts of the pupil's body and transfers power to it. Occasionally the rite of nyasa is performed by the guru simply looking at the chela and mentally charging him with power. Then comes the rite of 'besprinkling' *(abhisheka)*, or the aspersion of the candidate with water.

Finally, he is given the name and details of his own personal deity *(yidam)*, who is known only to the guru, and now also to the chela. The yidam is generally a particular facet, or personified power-aspect of one of the major deities of the sect, with emphasis on those features that are thought to be of special relevance to the chela.

The chela now has a formula for repetition, a ritual for practice, and a deity for personal worship.

In some tantrik initiation ceremonies there may be variant or supplementary features. Thus, in some cases a woman will assist at the initiation, for certain kinds of esoteric knowledge can only be communicated through the goddess or in the presence of her representative, who must be a woman. This may be followed by a rite of sexual intercourse between the pupil and the woman.

Again, sometimes the liquid used to besprinkle the pupil may be the blood of a newly sacrificed goat or black cock. The chela may be gashed on the right arm and some of the blood smeared on the statue of the goddess. He may also be branded on the thigh, breast or buttocks with a hot iron. Psychological horrors attend certain forms of initiation, in which the candidate has encounters with demons and the spirits of the dead.

When the rite of initiation has been completed, the candidate is regarded as a *vira* or hero, as distinguished from the *pashu* or animal herd, that is, the uninitiated rest of humanity.

Idols
During the ceremony of initiation, and indeed all the major tantrik ceremonies, the idol of the cult deity and his consort are

in evidence, for they must be present to witness the admission of the candidate into the community of tantriks.

Large sections of tantrik texts are devoted to the making of images, their installation, consecration and enlivenment, and the various ceremonies attending their worship. The materials used are selected with care. Figures made of clay are destroyed after use. Others are made of more durable material, such as stone or metal, and housed in little shrines or elaborate temples.

All idols are made according to certain set canons of proportion. Their size is precisely fixed for each purpose. The stance of the idol, the number of heads or arms it has, the objects held in the hands, the vehicle on which the idol is mounted, all are determined by precise norms. The selection of the site where the idol is to be installed, the laying down of the foundation, the setting up of the image, are all likewise matters of ancient tradition.

The most important part of the procedure is the so-called enlivening of the figure, and the technique followed is remarkably similar to that found in other earlier cultures. The ancient Egyptians enlivened their idols in a ceremony known as *upt-ro*, 'opening the mouth', that was performed not only for idols, but also for images of the dead, and for mummies at the funeral rites.

Relics of this custom survived in Graeco-Roman Egypt till the early centuries of the present era. It was then referred to by the Greek term *theopoea*, 'god-endowing', a magical rite which caused the power of the deity to become imprisoned within an idol properly made and duly installed. The Neoplatonists of Alexandria (c. A.D. 250) were acquainted with the technique but regarded it as an evil and dangerous art.

In Tantrism the ceremony of enlivening an idol is called *prana-pratishtha*, 'life-implacing', and is always performed on an auspicious day and at an astrologically determined hour. By the incantation of mantras, magical gestures, besprinkling and naming, the life-qualities of the deity are drawn down to reside in the image, which is thereafter worshipped as if it were the deity itself. The idol is treated not merely as an aid to meditation, but as the divinity manifest.

From then on the power of the idol is thought to be sustained and enhanced by being tended and worshipped. In Tantrism, worship proceeds by certain ritually prescribed phases: the deity is invoked, bells are rung, incense burned, lights waved, flowers offered, food served. The deity is then formally worshipped by prostrations, after which it is ritually dismissed.

Aesthetics

The making of idols in Hinduism is closely linked with religious architecture, for the larger idols were made for installation in the temples used for public worship. This again, is connected with the arts of sculpture and painting, and with music and the dance.

Although the arts have a long history in the Indian religions, the orthodox sects were always careful to insist that their function and application be carefully controlled, for it was realized that the untrammelled expression of sensuous forms had its dangers. Several Hindu lawgivers placed under total condemnation any work of art that was likely to excite undue admiration or pleasure because of the beauty of its outward form. The Jains also warned about being deluded and enticed by pleasing forms in art and writing into accepting ugly beliefs and evil doctrines.

Buddha himself opposed the presentation of his teachings in alluring sensuous guise, whether literary or pictorial. Buddhist legend tells of the monk Chittagutta who lived in a monastery for sixty years and never once lifted up his eyes to look at the magnificent murals depicting scenes from the life of Buddha, in case he took too sensuous a delight in their beauty. The Buddhist writer Buddhaghosha (fl. A.D. 430) denounced all painters and musicians as purveyors of meretricious luxuries.

Tantrism took a different view. All the arts, including music, were raised to sublime degree in the catalogue of tantrik skills. Beauty, it was said, appeals to the emotions, stimulates the creative faculties, and enriches the senses. The tantrik saint can be a thorough-going aesthete and hedonist. He is described as stupified with wine, sitting on embroidered satin cushions, surrounded by works of art, feasting on spiced meats. He makes music on his lute, singing poems of his own composition. With him is a beautiful girl whose sexual embraces he repeatedly enjoys. All this in the service of the deity.

This attitude is also adopted in a more specifically religious context. Every temple banner becomes a religious pennant, every colourful image is an icon, and every step of the nautch-girl dancing in the temple courtyard an invitation to religious bliss. The tantrik dance, individual or collective, may represent the motions of sexual intercourse, or the corybantic frenzy of the milkmaids as they whirl around the god Krishna, or take on the vigorous gyrations of the masked mummers described by western observers as 'devil dancers'.

The languorous forms of tantrik sculptures, the voluptuous stances of the deities in their brightly coloured paintings, the rich designs of their mandalas are all mystical symbols depicting, for those who have eyes to see, the correspondence between things earthly and things divine.

Intensity

This philosophy of life is to be reinforced by the practice of augmenting the energy and violence of one's feelings and natural instincts. Burning ardour, strong passion, a mood of turbulent excitement, all these are powerful aids that make for a heightened consciousness, help to concentrate spiritual force, and lead to the liberation of self and ultimately to a state of union with the Absolute. The nature of the feeling is immaterial. It may be one of passionate devotion or raging lust, burning love or murderous hate.

One way of expressing this intensity is through the use of obscene language. Obscenity is the verbal counterpart of erotic sculpture, a form of linguistic sexuality and erotic aggression. During certain Hindu folk festivals, abusive language and improper gestures are part of accepted practice. But in Tantrism such speech and actions are deliberately cultivated. A rich vocabulary of scurrility, and a varied and suggestive miming of indecent acts, betoken progress in the cult.

The foulest language is used relating to sexual intercourse with another's wife, mother, sister or daughter, to sodomy and bestiality, to the male and female sexual attributes. This may be demonstrated by simulating the sexual act, by exposing the private parts and going through the motions of self-abuse, especially at the sight of young women, by defecating in public places and by the sound of breaking wind.

Earlier texts explicitly state that the goddess is gratified and propitiated by filthy words and coarse actions, and that those who seek to avoid such behaviour displease her (Desai, 1975, p.177). Even prayers and invocations may be couched in the coarsest terms, and at times nothing distinguishes the language of religious devotion from the language of sexual gratification.

Naturalism

It is a matter of common sense, say the tantriks, that nature cannot be transgressed, so whatever is natural *(sahaja)* cannot be wrong. They therefore call for the uninhibited life, free from the bondage of artificial convention and social restraint, and feelings of remorse and guilt. The tantrik would prefer to go about in a state of complete nudity, which is the natural condition, if restrictive social laws did not forbid it.

The bodily functions and the generative organs are blessings bestowed on us by the beneficent deities, and should be dedicated to them. Erection and emission, micturition and evacuation, should be modes of homage and worship. The most natural acts are the most meritorious: eating and drinking which sustain life; sexual gratification which propagates it; and the natural functions which give it ease.

There is no 'moral' implication in these functions, and all should be allowed their due fulfilment. Sex is an amoral activity to which evil is not applicable. It is no more evil than eating, drinking, sleeping or drawing breath, and should not be subject to the jurisdiction of the family, society or state. Tantriks maintain that the current codes of morality are unnatural and injurious. Organized society, religion and law are inimical to the *sahajiya* or 'naturalist' doctrine.

Tantriks regard themselves as an élite who are above the moral and social laws that govern the *pashu* or herd. To them nothing is prohibited and all things are permissible. Therefore, one of the first things needful for the initiate into Tantrism is for him to be weaned as soon as possible from the traditional standards of morality. He must first learn to become indifferent to the traditional taboos. He must then positively reject them. And finally, he must become actively hostile to them.

When the laws of social morality cease to apply, as a result of the tantrik's transvaluation of them, he is ready to adopt and embrace the amoral life of the other members of the cult. He is ready to rise above the conventional law. What others condemn he assumes as a badge of nobility and superior status. What poisons others nourishes him. What sends the herd to hell ensures his salvation. Prohibited acts are the rungs of a ladder by which he ascends to the heights.

The distinctions made between what is right and what is wrong are abolished. When opposites unite, imbalance and tension are removed. There are no dualities any more, only a mystical union, for all things are one. In Tantrism all opposites are believed to be reconciled, since all opposites and contraries are illusory. This identification of polar opposites is a variant of the Eastern philosophy of non-differentiation and unity.

The self and what it seeks are one. This is expressed in the ancient saying *aham brahmasmi*, 'I am Brahma (or God)'. There is neither deity nor devotee, for God and worshipper are identical. Down the line the whole set of conflicting opposites is likewise abandoned. There is neither affirmation nor denial, neither here nor there, neither form nor formlessness.

No distinction is to be made between good and evil. There is no virtue and there is no vice. Folly and wisdom are one, for the folly of fools is wisdom, and the wisdom of the wise folly. There is no difference between jewel and husk, prince and pauper, slave and master, brahmin and untouchable. There is no difference between industry and idleness, pleasure and pain, praise and scorn, honour and dishonour. Tantriks deliberately court situations that invite scorn, blame and ridicule, and expose themselves to odium and abuse. He who is despised, they say, is freed from all attachment.

Forbidden sexuality, including incest and adultery can and indeed must be practised. Meats like beef, taboo to the Hindu, must be eaten. Alcoholic liquor, so hateful to the orthodox, must be drunk. A tantrik precept says, 'By drinking and drinking and drinking again, rolling on the ground, rising and still drinking, a man saves himself from rebirth' (Chaudhuri, 1979, p.250). 'Wine', says the *Mahanirvana Tantra*, 'is the goddess herself in liquid form, the mother of enjoyment and liberation.'

There is neither purity nor impurity, neither clean nor unclean. There is no difference between food and offal, between fruit juice and blood, between vegetable sap and urine, between syrup and semen. Among tantriks of extreme sects, scatological

substances and even human flesh are actually consumed as part
of a ritual symbolizing the end of these distinctions, and the
rejection of all the traditional values imposed by habit, convention and acquired taste.

Antinomianism

In India, tantriks belong to what are termed the left *(vama)* or
sinistral sects, in contradistinction to the followers of the right-
hand path, who observe the orthodox practices. The fact that
the term *vama* means both 'left' and 'woman', underlines the
important role assigned to the female in left-hand sects. In
almost all the Indian vernaculars, the term *vama-chara*, 'left-hand
path', implies fornication.

A characteristic feature of tantrik ritualism, both in India
and Tibet, is 'opposite-doing' *(viparit-karani)*, the carrying out of
certain actions contrary to normal practice. In the *vama* sects,
things ordinarily considered unclean and disgusting, such as the
excretions of the human body, are employed in certain cult
rites. Ritual copulation takes place in 'reversed order', the
woman being superincumbent during the act, or else coitus is
performed *in ano*, as this is regarded as abnormal and tantrik,
and therefore draws down more perverse powers, and makes
more potent magic.

In Tibetan Tantrism sacrifices are dedicated and offered to
'all spirits, demons, goblins, wicked spirits, spirits of insanity
and epilepsy'. As Sierksma says, Tibet is a country 'where devils
bring salvation'. In the Tibetan epic about the exploits of the
fierce and warlike Gesar of Ling (c. A.D. 780) it is stated, 'Gods
too are demons' (Sierksma, 1966, p.25).

The ranks of the tantrik hierarchy are frequently augmented
by heretical and apostate priests. Their saints and most eminent
hierophants are magicians, sorcerers and necromancers, and are
revered in proportion to their power to do maleficia and evil.

In the left-hand sects, the implements used, the rituals
adopted, and the methods of practising them, are contrary to
those approved by the orthodox canon, and many indeed are
expressly forbidden. One tantrik text, the *Rudra-yamala* (c. A.D.
1000), prescribes a rosary with beads made of human teeth, a
bowl made of a man's skull, a mat made of human skin, a
bracelet made from the hair of a female corpse, and intercourse

with a woman who is not one's wife.

The wheel of the Bon priests of Tibet has thirteen divisions instead of the usual twelve, and is turned leftward and not right. The Bon and other unorthodox sects of Tibet turn their sacred objects not in a dextral (clockwise) but in a sinistral (anti-clockwise) direction. S. K. R. Rao points out that the arms of the Bon swastika are turned in the opposite direction to the swastika of the Buddhist. Circumambulations are performed leftward or counterclockwise. Sacred chants are recited in reverse order. The Buddhist mantra, 'mani padme hum', is uttered backwards, 'muh-em-pad-ni-mo' (Rao, 1977, p.8).

In tantrik philosophy all acts are regarded as neutral. It does not matter whether they are good or evil in the usual under-standing of these terms. The same idea is also found reflected in some of the earliest scriptures of Hinduism. The *Brihad-aranyaka Upanishad* says, 'One who has this knowledge [of Brahma], although he commits great evils, becomes pure and immortal'. In the *Bhagavad-gita*, the god Krishna, counselling Arjuna to slay his relations and friends, says, 'He who has no feeling of self, even though he kills all these people, does not really kill'.

Among the many antinomian sayings found in tantrik writings the following are relevant in the present context. The *Kularnava Tantra* says, 'Those evil deeds that cause a man to burn in hell are the same as those by which the yogi attains salvation'. In the *Advaya-vajra Samgraha*, a Buddhist tantrik work, we read: 'By the very acts through which the ordinary person boils in a terrible hell for one hundred million aeons, by those very acts does the initiate yogi obtain emancipation'.

'A wise man', says the *Hevajra Tantra*, 'should remove the filth of his mind by filth'; and, 'One must rise by that through which one falls'. And again, 'As flatulence is cured by eating beans so that wind may expel wind, as a thorn in the foot can be removed by another thorn, and as poison can be neutralized by poison, so sin can purge sin'.

The tantrik is led by his natural instincts to what is pleasurable, and pleasure is a pathway to salvation. 'Do not suppress your feelings', he is told in the *Guhya-samaja Tantra*, 'choose whatever you want, and do whatever you desire, for in this way you please the goddess. Perfection can be attained by satisfying all one's desires.'

Hence such maxims as *mukti* through *bhukti* (salvation through sensuality), and *yoga* through *bhoga* (union with God through sexual enjoyment). A modern exponent of Tantrism, Acharya Shree Rajneesh says, 'The journey to Kama [erotic love] is also to Rama [God]; the journey to lust is also to light' (Colaabavala, 1980, p.46).

2.

TANTRIK PHYSIOLOGY

The Body

In tantrik physiology the human body and its functions are linked to the greater universe around us, for the human being is seen as a microcosm containing in essence all the energies of the cosmos. The universe and man are interrelated and each part of the cosmos is thought to have its counterpart in man. The galaxies and stars, sun and moon, all the elements of the earth, and all places of pilgrimage are contained within him. Likewise, the interplay of all the opposites, good and evil, activity and passivity, male and female, knowledge and action, growth and decay, are to be found reflected in man.

Central to the cosmic scheme and forming the axis around which the universe revolves is Mount Meru, of Asian mythology. In the human body this axis has its counterpart in the spine. And the other cosmographical features, the heavenly dome, the circular pathways of the constellations, the cosmic mountains and rivers, have their analogues in the cranium, the chakras, and the internal ducts and arteries that make up the complex of the human physiological system.

Buddha said to his disciples, 'I proclaim to you that this animated body, no more than one fathom high, is the dwelling place of the world'. In the *Vishvasara Tantra* we read, 'What is here is elsewhere. What is not here is nowhere.' Another text has it: 'He who realizes the truth of the body can come to know the truth of the universe'.

The tantriks say that man is placed in a physical environment so that he might make the best use of it for his own advancement. He is given sensual appetites for the furtherance of his spiritual aspirations. The soul can best be served through the body. The body is the vehicle for the soul's emancipation, and the cultivation of the body is therefore of prime importance to the tantrik.

Yoga

The discipline that is directed to the control of body, mind and spirit is called *yoga*, a term of broad significance which, like tantra, means method, way, technique or study. In this sense there are dozens of yogas, such as: *raja yoga*, concerned with spiritual culture; *bhakti yoga*, with salvation through faith; *guru yoga*, salvation through devotion to the guru; *jnana yoga*, enlightenment through knowledge; *karma yoga*, the way of action or works; *shilpa yoga*, the way of the artist, the technique of drawing mandalas and fashioning idols; *shabda yoga*, the yoga that studies sound and its effects; *mantra yoga*, which studies specifically the value of mantras and spells; *japa yoga*, still more specifically concerned with the value of repeating such spells.

Each kind of yoga has a series of stages through which the aspirant must proceed step by step, some requiring a progression through as many as eighteen stages. The chief stages of yoga, whatever its form, can be reduced to four, namely: (1) external conduct, including ritual observance; (2) self control, or internal discipline; (3) knowledge and control of the physical body and its functions; and (4) mental and spiritual control through meditative exercises.

Perhaps the most commonly practiced form of yoga, and one which the tantrik is principally concerned with mastering, is *hatha yoga*, or physical culture, the basic principles of which were first laid down by the semi-historical master, Matsyendra (d. A.D. 800). Its main disciplines include: the *asanas* or physical postures; *pranayama* or breathing exercises; the activation of the *chakras* or plexuses (the study of which is called *laya yoga*); and in particular, the activation of the *kundalini*, the lowermost plexus.

Among the objectives of hatha yoga is control over certain autonomic functions, that is, those not under the direction of the conscious mind, such as body temperature, the pulse rate, and the reflexes that cause erection and ejaculation, besides an overall control of the bodily apparatus, giving it strength and stamina to fit it for the strains of tantrik sexual practices, with the ultimate aim of achieving supernatural powers and making the body perfect and immutable.

Asanas

The *asana* or 'seat', is a generic name for a number of physical postures used in yogic meditative and occult practice where the yogi assumes a certain stance and arranges his limbs in various specified positions. Some tantriks regard the asana as an end in itself and believe that its mastery will confer all the powers that accrue from yoga in all its other forms. Some asanas are said to be good for health, and bestow longevity, youthfulness and sexual vigour. Some speed up the circulation of the internal currents and energize the body. Some alter the dynamic polarity of the body. Certain 'graveyard' asanas used in tantrik terror rites, to be described later, give one power over demonic forces.

Most of the asanas are motionless, and while the limbs are fixed in the prescribed attitudes, internal exercises are carried out. In each case the torsions of the body are said to represent a particular occult pattern and magical symbol, so that the body becomes a living talisman, charged with the desired potency.

The asanas are symbolically named after a plant, tree, bird or animal, or some object like the bow or plough. Others are descriptively named, like the hand-toe posture, the feet-head posture, the knee-touching posture, and so on. The commonest is the lotus posture *(padma-asana)*, the ordinary cross-legged squat, which has a number of variations.

The idea of turning upside down in order that the forces within the body might be realigned, was in consonance with the tantrik predilection for turning things topsy-turvy, and numerous asanas were devised to this end. One of the best known is the *shirsha-asana*, where the practitioner stands on his head, and thus reverses the natural order of his normal erect stance. There are over one hundred variations of the headstand.

The purpose of the headstand is to change the direction of the secret rivers and tributaries in the subtle or etheric body so that they flow towards the hidden caverns and reservoirs of the brain. While anyone can stand on his head, the control of the energy currents along the desired channels is a difficult and entirely different matter, known only to a few. In Tantrism this technique is transmitted in secret from master to pupil. It should never be attempted without guidance, for as with most occult operations it can be full of hazards.

The first effect of the headstand correctly executed is described as 'chaos', resulting from the unnatural physiological, and therefore psychological, position. By special concentration procedures the chaos gradually subsides and resolves itself into an ordered pattern whereby the potencies of the lower plexuses, the testes, the anus and the pubic fascia, are conjoined to flow toward the nuptial chambers of the brain. There, in esoteric terms, a union is enacted between the lower and upper potencies, when the fluidic energies are 'set on fire' and a state of bliss and illumination supervenes.

The headstand is also used for other purposes. Thus, one variant of this asana is employed for direct spermepotation, or the imbibing of is own semen by the yogi thus positioned. Among the coital postures of tantrik sex magic is the reversed way, in which the woman stands upside down, while the man stands upright beside her and 'sips' her female energy. Taoist manuals recommend several kinds of headstand, among them one called 'hanging like a bear', which is a method of 'making the semen ascend' in order to invigorate the brain. Another one, performed in combination with respiratory and cardiac control, reveals the 'secret of the bat', giving one the power of levitation and flying through the air, and also of astral travel.

Mudras

The word *mudra* is used in Tantrism, sometimes for the cereal that is eaten during the ritual feast, sometimes for the sexual positions assumed by the female partner, and sometimes for the female partner herself. More specifically, the mudra is a gesture formed by a certain positioning and interweaving of the fingers of one or both hands. Mudras are used in dancing, meditation, devotions and ritual worship, and play an important part in many tantrik rites.

The one-hand mudras are variations of four basic hand-positions, namely: the open palm, the cupped hand, the hand with the fingertips touching, and the closed fist. In each case the fingers may be arranged in different ways. In the two-handed mudras the hands may be separate or joined together to make various symbolical configurations: the tortoise, lion, lotus, bee, and so on.

Some mudras are formed for blessing (the benediction

mudra), others for enjoyment (the pleasure-giving mudra), for cursing (the wrathful-fist gesture), for warning (the threatening-finger gesture). Many express sexual symbols, the phallus, the vulva and the two in union in their infinite diversity. The mudra is in effect a manual asana, and the twists and contortions of the limbs during the bodily stance can be replicated in the mudra by the flexing and coiling of the fingers. The powers drawn down by the larger symbol of the body in its magical positions can likewise be embodied within the lesser configurations of the hands.

Pranayama

Perhaps the most important single feature of hatha yoga is *pranayama* or breath control. Respiratory exercises and the mastery of breathing techniques provide the key to the yogi's physical and mental health and vigour. The basic training relates to: (a) inhalation, (b) retention of the indrawn breath, (c) exhalation, and (d) holding still after exhalation.

The duration of each inhalation, retention, exhalation and holding phase is measured in units of time (today, in seconds) and exact ratios have been worked out for breathing in ordered and rhythmic sequence, with the object of obtaining different desired results. There are specific ratios for curing specific diseases, and for giving strength to the various parts of the body. This is usually done during the retention phase after inhalation, when the pneumic current is sent to the organ concerned to be healed or energized.

Tantrik adepts bring their knowledge of pranayama to bear during the sex magical rites, usually with the assistance of a suitably trained partner. In Taoist belief, the woman's breath during satisfactory intercourse is charged with *yin* essence, and the male practitioner can rejuvenate himself by inhaling this breath as it is discharged. But to do this effectively requires special training, and not everyone can make use of it. Tantriks also practice conspiration, or 'co-breathing', with their sexual partners, resulting in their united breath developing a high degree of potency, which can then be used for magical purposes (Walker, 1977, p.64).

Advanced pranayama is also concerned with the stabilizing of breath, since this is connected with the control of semen. The

Goraksha Samhita states, 'So long as the breath is in motion the semen moves. When the breath ceases to move the semen is also at rest'. Such cessation of breath is not the simple retention of breath as might be thought, but an extremely difficult and secret technique of stilling the movement of breath within the body. This, in turn linked with the great mystery of total thought-control, produces a climactic state which, if reached, is said to put the most extraordinary powers within the grasp of the yogi.

Much tedious and exacting preparation concerned with breath-control during pranayama, the retention of semen during coition, and stillness of mind during meditation, must be undergone before these three features are brought at last into simultaneous operation in a special manner to achieve the stabilization of breath, semen and consciousness during the sex act, and so attain a form of unifying mystical experience of oneness in duality. In the *Guhya-siddhi* we read, 'Let the aspirant insert the phallus *(linga)* into the vulva *(bhaga)*, but not discharge the wisdom-mind *(bodhi-chitta)*'. Texts dealing with these matters are contained in a number of Tantras, and there is an enormous esoteric commentary on them.

Chakras

Generally translated 'plexus', the *chakra* is a vortex or pulse-point of psychic energy in the subtle or etheric body at its point of contact with the physical body. Each chakra is a centre for the supply and distribution to the physical body of the life-bearing etheric forces. The chakras thus constitute a part of the secondary somatic system, where the vitalic and psychic energies crystallize into physical qualities.

Belief in the chakras has been remarkably widespread. Besides India, it was current among the ancient Egyptians, the peoples of the early Middle East, the Chinese, and even the Mayas of Central America. The diffusion centre for the Western hemisphere may have been ancient Egypt, whence the idea probably passed, by way of the Hellenistic kingdoms and Byzantium, to the Sufis of the Islamic world, and eventually to the Christian Hesychast monks of fourteenth-century Greece.

In the Hindu system there are said to be 88,000 chakras in the human body, each one forming the junction point of a number of subtle arteries *(nadis)* that ramify throughout the body. Yogic practitioners name thirty chakras situated in such parts as the big toe, the knee, the groin, the tip of the nose. But of these only seven are considered to be of supreme importance, and these are situated along the central axis of the subtle anatomy that passes from tailbone to skull.

The seven major chakras are depicted in drawings as circular shapes, representing lotuses of variegated colour, each with a certain number of petals. Each chakra is associated with a letter of the Sanskrit alphabet, a syllabic sound (mantra), a musical note, geometrical figure, physical element, an animal, a part of the body, a sense organ, a vital breath, a male deity, a female deity, a demon and demoness, and so on.

Listed below are the seven main chakras of the tantrik system.

(1) *Sahasrara*, 'thousand-petalled', situated in the crown of the head. Its associated plexus, the cerebral, bregmic or ventricular plexus. Associated endocrine gland, the pituitary. Distilled and precipitated from the sahasrara is a fluid, which is stored within the ventricles or hollow chambers of the brain. This forms what is called *rasa*, 'juice', or the elixir of immortality. Ordinarily the fluid passes down into the nasal passages, becomes contaminated and goes to waste. The object of certain tantrik exercises is to prevent the loss of this precious fluid, to conserve and utilize it, and ultimately to effect a union of the elixir with the fire force of the kundalini (see below).

(2) *Ajna*, 'understanding', situated between the eyebrows, but extending inwards. Associated plexus, the glabella in the forehead. Endocrine gland, pineal.

(3) *Vishuddha*, 'pure', situated in the region of the throat. Plexus, pharyngeal or laryngeal. Endocrine gland, thyroid.

(4) *Anahata*, 'new', situated in the heart. Plexus, cardiac. Endocrine gland, thymus.

(5) *Manipura*, 'gem-site', situated between the breastbone and the navel. Plexus, epigastric or solar. Endocrine glands, adrenals.

(6) *Svadishthana*, 'pleasant', situated in the pubic region. Plexus, hypogastric, or pubic fascia. Endocrine gland, pancreas.

(7) *Muladhara*, 'root-foundation', or base chakra, situated in the perineum, between the anus and the genitals. Plexus,

perineal body or sacral plexus. Endocrine glands, gonads (ovaries or testes). Many important subtle arteries are rooted in the muladhara.

Kundalini

The muladhara chakra is also the site of a mysterious energy called *kundalini*, which is likened to a tiny snake, or a spiral of fire-energy, lying 'coiled' *(kundala)* and asleep near the tailbone. The sahasrara and kundalini are occult opposites. The sahasrara is fluid, the kundalini is flame. The sahasrara is male, the kundalini female. The sahasrara is the quintessence of Shiva, the kundalini the quintessence of Shakti.

The chakras are sometimes compared to focuses of occult fire, lying dormant. In the kundalini there flickers an incendiary point, normally quiescent. A sympathetic resonance exists along the axis of the aligned chakras, which vibrate gently in mutual harmony.

The object of certain tantrik exercises is the arousal and ascent of the kundalini. By elaborate yogic techniques the ember of the kundalini is made to blaze up until the flame reaches the chakra above and ignites it. In this manner the fiery stream goes from chakra to chakra until it reaches the sahasrara or crown plexus at the top of the head. The kundalini is thus said to pierce the gates of the chakras one by one until it ascends to the summit.

Strange physical sensations accompany the arousal and ascent of the kundalini. Curious phenomena of light and sound are experienced by the practitioner. He hears the roar of an ocean, the thunder of a waterfall, the tinkling sound of bells, the hum of bees. He becomes dizzy, and then there is silence. This is followed by a visual kaleidoscope of dots of light, flames of fire, coloured lines, dazzling geometrical shapes.

Experts warn that very real dangers attend the arousal of the kundalini. It takes many years to master, under the personal guidance of a guru, and should therefore not be undertaken unless one has been trained to deal with it. The fire force if uncontrolled can cause serious physical and phychological damage that may lead to insanity and even death. But words fail to describe the climax of the operation when the kundalini successfully reaches the sahasrara, and Shakti is united with

Shiva. It is the Great Awakening, the Immortal Draught, the Supreme Bliss *(Mahasukha)*.

In the tantrik view, since both male and female potencies reside within the body, each person can unite with himself by raising the kundalini to the sahasrara. A number of modern practitioners have spoken in exalted terms of this consummation. 'What need have I of any outer woman?' the yogi says, 'I have an inner woman within myself' (Mookerjee, 1971, p.114).

Paramudra

The interior structure of the etheric body and its operations is represented in a chart showing the vitalic currents that flow through the *nadis* (ducts) of the psychosomatic system, and the knots that dam the flow at certain critical bends and twists. Yoga has devised a series of postures and exercises to control the flow of these currents by internal contraction of a muscle or organ that serves as a knot *(bandha)* at the required point.

The *paramudra* or 'supreme posture', also called a *mahamudra*, 'great posture', is a combination of a bodily attitude *(asana)*, breath control *(pranayama)*, hand gesture *(mudra)*, the lock *(bandha)*, and meditation on mystical syllables *(mantras)*, which are concerted into a single dynamic operation to convert the body into a grand talismanic symbol.

There are said to be eighty-eight great mudras in all, each one having a specific occult purpose, and each entailing the locking of a sense organ; or some part of the body, the throat, heart, abdomen, phallus; or some bodily orifice; or some tube or channel; and bringing under control the energy-bearing chakras connected with them.

One preparatory mahamudra involves sealing the nine gates of the body, namely: the mouth (1), the ears (2), the eyes (2), the nostrils (2), penis (1) and anus (1). This insulates the body against external interference, strengthens its resistance and converts it into an instrument of power.

In another such mudra the tongue is turned backwards into the gullet to block the orifices of the nasal passage that open into the mouth. By 'closing the tenth gate' in this manner, the nectar from the plexus at the crown of the head, the sahasrara, is prevented from dripping downwards unutilized.

Again, the head is bent forward and the chin pressed down as far as it will go towards the triangular hollow at the join of the collar bones, thereby constricting the network of arteries situated there. This seals off the subtle arteries that connect the head with the rest of the body.

There is said to be a major *nadi* or duct running down the interior of the spinal column, called the *sushumna*, along which the vital pranic currents travel, and from which they ramify through the rest of the body. On either side of this main channel are two subsidiary ducts, the one on the left called the *ida*, and the one on the right the *pingala*. Lesser currents of the pranic stream are believed to pass up and down these lesser ducts. By contracting the muscles of the anus the two subsidiary ducts are blocked off, the pranic current is forced back into the central column, and this assists in the arousal of the kundalini.

In the phallic lock, the phallus is made erect and hard, and then locked for an indefinite period while in this 'adamantine' state. The condition is further assisted by recourse to aphrodisiacs and drugs. In rites of mystic sexuality, the tantrik adept remains locked with his female partner while certain internal exercises, both sexual and meditative, are carried out. Because of the debilitating effect it has on the woman, the tantrik sometimes uses more than one partner for this purpose.

The paramudra for the 'arrest and stabilization of semen' is used in conjunction with certain exercises that enable the practitioner to retain his semen, retard ejaculation, and prolong coitus, in order to effect a transmutation of his physical, mental and supernatural faculties. This is sometimes done in association with *oli* techniques to be mentioned later.

It is to be noted that all such practices are extremely complex. The anal lock, for instance, is much more than a simple contraction of the anal sphincter, but is a psychophysical operation taking many months to perfect. The parmudras are never fully described in writing, being very dangerous to execute. Some are only hinted at, and not even named.

According to Tantrik tradition, the paramudras are concerned not only with the physical and subtle bodies, but even with one's future bodies, and require the aid of demons, demonesses and other elemental beings. Wrongly done they could harm the practitioner for several future incarnations.

But to those who perform them with care and under the

guidance of a competent guru, the texts promise 'immunity from hunger, swooning, sloth, disease and death'. The practitioner will become irresistibly attractive to women. He will be freed from all past sin. He will become sinless even if he commits a thousand murders or countless adulteries in future. He will become immortal. He will wander with delight through the twenty-one worlds, and will remain unharmed even at the time of the universal dissolution.

Siddhi

The Tantrik adept claims to be a person possessing not only knowledge and enlightenment, but also *siddhi* or supernatural power. Extraordinary magical gifts of this kind are held out to those who acquire proficiency in the more difficult yogic arts.

According to Patanjali (c. A.D. 500), author of an early treatise on yoga, siddhis come as a result of natural endowment, drugs, spells, austerities and meditation. Tantriks make use of drugs, practice austerities, and have their own mantras and forms of meditation. The siddhis claimed by them are attained largely as a result of occult techniques.

The person who possesses siddhi is known as a *sadhu*, although this term is popularly applied to many kinds of ascetic wonder-worker. More accurately, the man with siddhi is a *siddha*, and although tradition speaks of a million siddhas (Rao, 1977, p.36), only eighty-four are recognized and enumerated, some historical, and all obscured in myth.

Another class of siddhi-achiever is the *natha*, 'lord', one who has reached a high stage of occult development, possesses supernatural powers, and is a supreme master of esoteric science and philosophy. Hindu and Buddhist tradition relating to these two groups, the siddhas and nathas, is extremely confused, and commonly little distinction is made between them. The vernacular literature relating to their feats goes back more than a thousand years.

There are all sorts of supernatural siddhis, and all in all they embrace every fanciful aspiration the soul could conceive. Kingly attributes are available to the lowly, and power to the powerless. There is the ability to reduce oneself to the size of an atom, or expand to the dimensions of the cosmos; to become as light as a cobweb, or as heavy as the Himalayas; to be transported anywhere in a flash; to raise the dead to life; to become invisible, invincible, clairvoyant, clairaudient, rich beyond dreams. One siddhi confers 'irresistible eloquence that renders opponents answerless'.

Actual siddhis have been claimed by numerous modern workers in this field, namely: control over fire, resistance to extreme cold, levitation, trance-walking at superhuman speed, the creation of thought-forms, and the suspension of respiration for prolonged periods.

Sexual siddhis are among the most commonly listed of all. Success with women and the ability to satisfy any number of them was the most coveted goal of many aspirants. This woman-subduing power was aimed at reducing females to a state of insane and demonic desire that only the tantrik could assuage. Women could be tormented beyond endurance so they would come in hundreds, with dishevelled locks, their bodices bursting with ardour, their garments slipping off with desire, their limbs atremble, and thirsting for the embraces of the tantrik, however decrepit, old, ugly or impotent he might be.

On a more transcendental level, these siddhis included the ability to have congress with beings on other planes of existence. Legend speaks of the phenomenal prowess of some stalwarts who assailed the gates of heaven, and then descended to the nether regions, to satisfy the sexual appetites of the female denizens of heaven and hell.

There is the power to enjoy the embraces of any mortal woman, past, present and future; the power to create beings according to one's particular needs, so that they will serve one sexually in any manner; the power of changing one's form to that of an animal, so that one might enjoy intercourse with animals, 'in the bestial mode'.

One siddhi called *para-pura-kaya-pravesha*, 'the transcendently-satisfying-body-occupying', enables the siddha to enter into the body of another man in order to enjoy his wives. A minor siddhi enables one to seduce with impunity any virgin one wishes to have.

Again, since a single individual could never really have enough of sexual delight, he could aim for the siddhi to multiply his body, as the god Krishna did, and simultaneously have intercourse with hundreds of women.

The siddhis pertaining to the dimensions and capacity of the male organ are equally astounding.

In order that one might enjoy to the full the benefits of all these extraordinary blessings, there is the siddhi that bestows on one the power of perpetual rejuvenation and longevity. And just in case something might have escaped the scope of this catalogue, an ultimate, all-comprehending siddhi embracing omniscience and omnipotence is listed, in which all conceivable possibilities and impossibilities may be realized.

3.

TANTRA AND SEX

Asceticism

Tantrism is generally anti-ascetic, but in certain circumstances asceticism is counted among the basic virtues and advocated as a means of salvation, enlightenment and power.

In its more rigid sense, asceticism implies renunciation of home and personal possessions and of family and social ties. It also implies austerity. The disciplines adopted by an ascetic may be quite arduous, requiring the employment of disagreeable, difficult, unnatural and often painful means for the attainment of the desired ends.

Solitude, silence and inactivity are essential to most kinds of asceticism. In Tibet, the monks belonging to sects like the Kargyud, borrowing from the Bon practice of immurement, will shut themselves up, sometimes for several months on end, behind what are called *tsams*, 'barriers', in mountain caves. The cave into which the hermit retires is walled up, and while in the cold and dark interior he will be allowed no contact with any human being. Food and water are regularly supplied to him through a small opening in the cave wall.

Asceticism has a long tradition in India. Legend speaks of the ancient rishis undergoing feats of the most heroic endurance, and causing consternation in heaven till the gods implore them to desist. The ash-besmeared sadhus of India, the chief exponents of asceticism, are both revered and dreaded for the powers they allegedly have as a result. They live in forest retreats far from the haunts of men. Some sit immobile in one place, day and night, summer and winter, never stirring except to eat a few morsels, and drink, and answer the calls of nature. Some sit with arm upraised until the arm atrophies. Some look upwards to the sky until their neck muscles harden. Some lie on a bed of thorns or nails.

Another essential feature of asceticism is continence, which strictly means the avoidance of all sexual activity. The Hindu lawgiver Manu (c. A.D. 200) said, 'Irresistible power comes from chastity'. In his book of yoga aphorisms, Patanjali writes, 'A man gains great energy through continence'.

Numerous methods exist for bringing the sexual appetite under control, or for getting rid of it altogether. In Hindu legend the god Shiva, having engendered enough progeny, decided on the path of asceticism and castrated himself (Sierksma, 1966, p.32). The Jains of India take a puritanical attitude to sex, and advocate chastity as a moral requirement. Some followers of this religion totally avoid sexual relations. In statues and pictures depicting their nude deities and saints, the penis is always shown hanging down in a flaccid state. The organs are intact, and the power conserved.

The objective of continence in Tantrism, however, is not the extirpation of sexual desire, and tantriks do not recommend such drastic expedients as castration. Nor is it the inhibition of the lower instincts and the conquest of sensuality, as the Jains would have it.

Tantriks distinguish between the continence of the true sadhu, which liberates the self, and the abnegation by the unenlightened person, which does not dam the stream of sexual desire, but only muddies it. The ultimate aim of tantrik asceticism is the generation within the body of the yogi of a kind of psychic glow, a condition known as *tapas*, a word which means both 'asceticism' and 'heat'.

The tantrik therefore employs not only the traditional methods of the ascetic, avoiding sex in all its forms, but may also undertake various kinds of erotic activity in order to arouse his sexual energy with the purpose of conserving it and making use of it for his own magical ends. This includes intercourse with the opposite sex, during which he absorbs energy from his female partner.

Gynergy

Although women are held in high esteem in Tantrism, they are regarded as dangerous within the context of some ascetic practices. Hence among certain sects of Tibet, such as the celibate Gelug-pa or Yellow Hats, homosexuality used to be very prevalent, sometimes even being regarded as a virtue, confirming as it were, that women no longer played any part in the life of those concerned. All evidence of the female sex was banned completely. The poultry yards of the Gesar temple in Lhasa contained only cocks.

Many Hindu saints past and present adopted an almost misogynous attitude to sex. 'There are three kinds of vice', declared the *Padma Purana* (c. A.D. 1100), 'but the most intoxicating is woman; there are seven kinds of poison, but the most venomous is woman'. The modern Hindu saint, Ramakrishna (d. 1886) considered 'women and gold' the great impediments to mystical experience and spiritual advancement.

Women, it is said, are natural psychic vampires who can sponge up male energy without effort. During invagination a woman magnetically draws in the male member, the male seed, and male psychic power, all at the same time. Women do not possess semen and are eager to receive it. Some women, by gluteal contraction of their genitals, will hold the penis in a firm grip that causes a vigorous erection, resulting in greater excitement and a copious discharge of the precious male fluid, to the detriment of the man. Tantrik neophtyes who fall into the hands of the wrong kind of *dakini* initiatrix can find themselves permanently depleted of their sexual vitality.

A tantrik expert on the other hand can exploit the woman for his own ends. Older tantriks make use of young women for rejuvenation. This arises from the belief in *gerocomy*, the idea that an older man can absorb vigour and youthfulness from a young woman. It is thought that during her orgasm a powerful current of gynergy, or female energy, surges through the woman, which the tantrik can learn to absorb by acclivity techniques. The man does not ejaculate, but takes in the orgasmic energy released by the woman each time he has intercourse with her.

In one curious rite of 'woman-worship' *(stri-puja)* the tantrik undertakes to serve a woman like a domestic for three months, progressing to more and more intimate relations with her. At first he sleeps in the same room with her, but on the floor, while she sleeps on the bed. After two weeks he joins her in bed, but at her feet; then beside her, but clothed. Then he lies beside her nude, fondling and caressing her. Then he has intercourse with her, but without emission. This is a form of 'closed' woman-worship, that is, without expending his semen. In this manner he builds up an inner tension, deliberately controlled by long self-discipline and complex yogic techniques, so that his physical system becomes a reservoir of psychic energy empowered by his restraint.

In this type of Tantrik sex practice, intercourse does not normally end in emission, and special techniques have been devised to prevent the loss of the precious male fluid. But the mere retention of the semen is not sufficient, for then it becomes stagnant and can be injurious. To the man who understands its value and virtues, it can become a source of illumination and power that can be turned to magical ends.

Semen

Tantrik continence is thus concerned primarily with the conservation and proper utilization of semen, the stream *(retas)* of life. The mystique of this fluid has been the subject of considerable commentary in the sexual literature of several Eastern countries. Arthur Waley (d. 1966), British authority on Chinese thought, points out that the Chinese word *p'o*, or 'physical soul', has an alternative meaning of 'semen'.

In Sanskrit writings the seminal essence is a concentrated source of energy, symbolized by a dot or point *(bindu)*. It is said to consist partly of reproductive liquids, and partly of a substance emanating from the crown plexus or sahasrara. Furthermore, it is believed to have varying properties, and in different circumstances can become a divine nectar *(amrita)*, a healing potion *(aushadha)*, or a deadly poison *(visha)*.

Knowledge of the properties of semen, and of the manner in which it can be conserved and utilized, are among the best guarded secrets of Tantrism. If the seed is emitted, the yogi falls under the law of time and mortality. On the other hand the yogi who can conserve his seed overcomes death, for death comes from the discharge of the bindu, and life is prolonged by its preservation. A Buddhist text reads, 'The seed *(bija)* must not fall. The falling of the seed leads to death. The keeping of the seed is life.' The sperm must be retained to replenish the brain and the psyche. The loss of semen is the loss of selfhood.

Strict asceticism and celibacy carried out in the prescribed manner sublimate the potencies of the male seed. The dross of the unexpended bindu is burned away by austerities and the residual pure essence is reabsorbed into the system. But a number of other techniques, which can here be mentioned only briefly, are concerned with the direct management of semen, either in normal intercourse or during autoerotic practice, so that its flow is directed inwards and upwards, into the yogi's own body and towards the cerebral plexus.

The Tantras state that the nectar of life should be absorbed by the yogi himself. 'The plough [penis] and the bulls [testes] the wise man will use for ploughing his own land and sowing his own seed, so that he can eat his own fruit.'

Various methods are recommended by which the yogi can 'eat his own fruit'. One is *coitus reservatus*, intercourse without ejaculation, which is widely practised by exponents of sexual magic the world over. In certain xenophrenic or trance-inducing exercises, the retention of semen is combined with the suspension of breath and of thought (see page 41).

In another method the yogi directs the seminal stream into himself. This is done by pressure on the perineum at the moment of climax, so that the fluid is intrajaculated direct into his own body (Walker, 1977, p.231). When combined with the 'upward-semen' *(urdhva-retas)* technique it is said to cause the energy of the inward-discharged semen to progress along the central channel of the subtle body through the stations of the chakras, to be transformed at the topmost chakra into the nectar of immortality.

The bindu may be discharged externally. In a gross form of spermepotation the yogi directs the discharged bindu into his own mouth during certain asanas, such as the headstand (see page 39). On various ritual occasions, such as initiation, chakrapuja and invigoration rites, the neophyte may also be required to ingest his own or his guru's semen.

Even when the bindu is discharged into the vagina the adept can transform it into a sacred substance. Then it becomes an offering, the purest form of sacrificial elixir, a pouring of oil upon the altar, that draws down the divine presence. In the *Hevajra Tantra* the god Hevajra says, 'I dwell in the vagina of the female in the form of semen'.

The seminal essence spreads an aura of magical power over

the whole arena of the pubic region and the vaginal canal. A medieval trantrik work, the *Karpura-adistotram*, promises that the man who offers a hair of his female partner plucked out by the root and soaked in his ejected semen, 'will become a great poet, and will go forth mounted on an elephant, to become lord of a realm'.

Finally, there is the process in which the tantrik discharges his energized semen at will in the normal way, but again only for the purpose of uniting his seed with the female 'ova-essence' of his partner by absorbing her energy through acclivity or 'ascent' (Walker, 1977, p.2). With his member still in position, he draws up through his penis the united essence (his seminal discharge and the female ova-essence) and absorbs it into his own system.

This constitutes one of the most secret *oli* methods (such as vajroli, amaroli and sahajoli), all of which require long and complicated exercises for developing phallic power. The word *oli* is a tantrik cult word of obscure origin meaning 'womb-fire', and the rationale of these techniques is explained only in part in such works as the *Hatha-yoga Pradipika* by Svatmarama Svamin (c. A.D.1430). Competence in these methods indicates a high grade of advancement in the tantrik's progress, and tantrik texts praise those enlightened people 'who are addicted to drinking the excellent nectar arising from sexual union'.

There are many other fanciful and improbable methods of doing things with semen, all extremely complex, and to the mind unused to the subject, disgusting in performance. Critics, both east and west, have condemned them in the strongest terms. Dr D. Chattopadhyaya refers to Tantrism as a corrupting and degrading religion, and speaks of tantrik practices as 'at once the most revolting and horrible that human depravity could think of'.

But to tantriks they are a legitimate way, enabling the practitioner to heighten his psychic and spiritual faculties and so gain mystical realization. The god Shiva, who is the master of all forms of sexual mysticism and sorcery, is represented as intoxicated with the elixir of immortality thus produced.

One of the chief aims of Tantrism is proficiency in those techniques that enable the aspirant to sublimate the sexual essences from the physical to the superphysical plane. Then, it is said, the whole being of the tantrik is revitalized, his skin glows, his body becomes radiant, and he is on the pathway to immortality.

Alchemy

Though semen is the most precious of the 'wet elements', it forms only one of a number of quintessential substances of magical quality employed in tantrik alchemy or *dhatu-vada*, 'substance-way'. These substances are both liquid and solid. The liquid substances include, besides semen, other bodily products such as saliva, milk, blood, faeces, urine, menses; the mysterious dew from the sahasrara or cerebral plexus; as well as liquids found in nature, such as water, sap, oils and juices.

A number of elements used in traditional alchemy are also employed by tantrik alchemists, among them mercury *(parada)*, which is regarded as the semen of Shiva, and mica *(abhra)* the ovum of Shakti, in addition to salt, sulphur, orpiment, bone-ash and metals of various kinds.

In Sanskrit, alchemy was also spoken of as *rasa-vada*, the term *rasa* meaning both 'liquid' and 'mercury', and scores of books, many still untranslated, were written on the virtues of the various rasas found internally and externally.

Some elements of alchemy were already known to the pre-Aryan aborigines of India, and much of this early knowledge was preserved in the treatises on *ayurveda*, the medical lore of ancient India. The principles of internal alchemy, concerned with the body, were introduced to India through Chinese sources; but the laboratory techniques of external alchemy came by way of the Arabs, who themselves inherited the basic ideas from Alexandria. Both internal and external alchemy, in spite of their foreign origins, took a typically Indian form. The search for the tincture of projection, longevity, youthfulness and immortality, combined alchemy with hatha yoga, breathing exercises, sexual magic and oli techniques. Alchemy became essentially a way of life, a mystic doctrine and a means of salvation.

In internal alchemy, the tantrik embarks on a course of exercises and experiments with and within the body, using his physical framework as a laboratory. Its objective is the transmutation, by yogic and magical means, of the substances inside himself.

External alchemy in India was concerned primarily with the preparation of medicinal remedies and herbal drugs; the under-

standing of poisons; the search for the philosopher's stone by
which baser metals are converted into gold; and the art of
preparing aphrodisiacs, something particularly desirable in the
polygynous households of princes and potentates who had a
large number of wives they had to keep contented.

Drugs were used in India from earliest times. The whole of
the ninth book of the *Rig-Veda* is devoted to the praise of a drink
called *soma*. This drink cannot be identified today although
several guesses have been made. In one opinion soma was con-
cocted from a hallucinogenic mushroom. In another, it was an
infusion of the hemp plant, or cannabis, or of the morning glory
creeper.

All drugs were dedicated to the god Shiva, who himself was
partial to them, especially cannabis. Many of Shiva's quarrels
with his wife Parvati, took place because he was prone to while
away aeons lost in a drug trance. Medieval Hindu texts declare
that liberation and occult power may be obtained through the
drugs, intoxicants, narcotics and other nostrums recommended
in alchemy. The Nathas, Siddhas, Rasavadas, and other allied
semi-tantrik sects, continually resort to drugs to shift the plane
of perception and attain ecstatic states and mystical illumination.

The intoxicant most commonly used was obtained from the
resin, leaves and stems of the hemp plant, now known as
hashish, cannabis or marijuana. The product, in its pure form
called *charas*, may be chewed as it is, or made into little pellets, or
else mixed with molasses and eaten as a sweet. It may be mixed
with sherbet and drunk as *bhang*. Or it may be dried or powdered
and inhaled like snuff or smoked as *ganja*.

Hashish induces euphoric and ecstatic moods, but sometimes
also leads to violent behaviour. It is regarded as the 'opposite' of
the calm-inducing opium. The Greek geographer Strabo (d. A.D.
21) mentions the Thracians taking hemp and then dancing
about in wild abandon. The Persian cult of the Assassins (c.
1200) get their name from hashish, because the cult leaders
resorted to cannabis to make their neophytes amenable to their
commands and willing to carry out acts of violence and murder.

Tantriks call canabis *vijaya*, 'victory', or *siddhi*, 'energy', and
frequently use it in their ceremonies. Since it is an aphrodisiac it
is taken preparatory to the celebration of chakrapuja (below).
'Tantriks use drugs', says Katinka Matson, 'to facilitate the

dissolving of ego and encourage the activity of meditation prior to sexual activity' (1979, p.327). In the male, hashish can produce a better erection and improve sexual performance, but will eventually result in the inhibition of ejaculation and of erection, and finally lead to impotence.

Menses

One of the most important among the many unique contributions that a woman makes to the 'wet elements' needed in alchemy is her menstrual blood *(rajas)*. According to the medieval alchemists of Europe, an essential ingredient for the philosopher's stone was to be found *in menstruo meretrices*, 'in the menses of a whore', and a similar idea prevailed in tantrik alchemy.

It is related that the brahmin alchemist Vyali (d. 1050) devoted many years without success in trying to distil the elixir of life. He had a prostitute to keep him company, and one day a drop of her menstrual blood fell into the mixture he was preparing. The mixture frothed up, and, with the additon of the precious 'mercury', provided by his own semen, he obtained the elixir he sought.

Menstruation is a distinctive attribute of the adult female. The *Matrika-bheda Tantra* names six types of menstrual flow, and other texts differentiate menses according to the type of woman, her caste and age, and also distinguish between the menses of a virgin, the first menses after marriage, the first menses after childbirth, the menses of a woman when she is reaching the end of her fertile life, as well as the menses on the first, second and third day of the flow at each of these life periods.

Since children are not normally conceived during menstruation, certain sects, like the Bauls of modern Bengal, practice 'sexual union without issue' by intercourse during menstruation. A child born as a result of such union is believed to be imbued with a very strong power, usually for evil. In legend, the god Vishnu in his boar incarnation mated with the earth goddess during her monthly periods, the offspring being the demon Naraka, one of the most vicious and licentious of his kind.

The interval between menstruations is known as *ritu*, the 'right' time for conception, when the woman is ready to receive the male sperm and her energy is directed to function as a mother-to-be. During her menstrual period, however, this powerful energy is freely available, and tantriks believe that it should not go to waste.

Menstruation is regarded by many Hindus as the time of a woman's impurity, and when she is menstruating she is generally segregated from the rest of the household and forbidden to participate in any of the domestic activities. She is treated as temporarily unclean. In Tantrism, the situation is reversed. A menstruating woman is put in a special category. During this time, her female energy is said to be at its highest, hence contact with her and her menstrual flow is considered invigorating and healthy.

The modern physiologist will say that a woman's menses consist of the disintegrated ovum, infertile blood, mucus, dead tissue, menotoxins and other poisonous substances. The tantrik retorts that this precious fluid is potent with ova energy and contains concentrations of tonic substances like arsenic, iron and lecithin.

Any woman in menses is the goddess incarnate and should be engaged in sexual rites in the appropriate manner. Philip Rawson says, 'The most powerful sexual rite of re-integration requires intercourse with the female partner when she is menstruating and her "red" sexual energy is at its peak' (1973, p.24). Menstrual blood is used in sex magic and alchemy, especially in the making of aphrodisiacs; and in the rites of chakrapuja the menses and semen of the participants may be taken as a ritual drink. Such potions are treated as the menstrual blood of Shakti and the seminal fluid of Shiva.

Sex in Religion
There are tantrik schools in India, Tibet, China and Japan that adopt a contemplative rather than a sexual approach to religion, and the sexual elements either receive little emphasis or are completely ignored. For example, in the Shingon sect of Japan, which is tantrik, the female bodhisattvas depicted in the mandalas are devoid of sexual attributes. In certain Chinese sects with a tantrik philosophical bias, sex receives hardly any mention at all. A few schools of Indian Tantrism likewise show an almost pharisaical attitude to matters of erotic interest, which precludes any sexual interpretation being given to their teachings.

Yet they are the exceptions, for most tantrik sects continue to emphasize the erotic aspects of Tantrism. They contend that concentration on matters of an erotic nature and the stimulation of the sexual feelings cause the psychic centres to become quickened in a special manner, leading to spiritual enlightenment. According to a modern writer, Tantrism says, 'Raise your enjoyment to its highest power, and then use it as a spiritual rocket fuel' (Rawson, 1973, p.9). Sex is a fact of existence, and one of the most basic of all human activities. It is a way of enjoying, prolonging and propagating life. Orgasm is a means of catharsis, and the sexual experience a method of Realization.

Sex has a venerable history in the Indian religious systems. The gods themselves are the great exemplars and instigators of sexual indulgence. The greatest of the tantrik deities, Shiva and Shakti, established sexuality and wished it to be perpetuated. Vishnu has a name that indicates his phallic origin, and certain treatises such as the *Yoni Tantra* have a strong Vaishnavite flavour (Schoterman, 1980, p.10).

Vishnu's chief avatar, the god Krishna, is an amorous deity, and the story of his life is filled with accounts of his erotic adventures. This blue-skinned deity consorted with virgins and married women, brahmin and low-caste females alike.

According to the tantriks, 'If sex is sinful, then there can be no greater sinner than God himself' (Colaabavala, 1980, p.50).

The ancient Vedic writings and philosophical treatises sometimes allude to the divine nature of the sexual act, and speak of worship in sexual terms. The *Brihad-aranyaka Upanishad* describes a sacrificial soma rite in which a woman was ritually transfigured to become a consecrated place for its performance: 'Her haunches are the sacrificial ground; her pubic region the altar; her pubic hairs the sacrificial grass; her moist labia the press of the soma plant; the red vulva the fire. Verily, great is the world for him who practices sexual intercourse while understanding the *vajapeya* ['vigour-draught'] sacrifice.'

The actual soma-pressing ceremony was accompanied by ritual intercourse between the sacrificer and his wife. According to the text: 'He knows the rite is woven upon the act of copulation. He summons. He makes a request. Together with the woman he lies down.' The successive stages of coition are made to coincide with the recitation of appropriate verses from the Vedic text by the officiating priest. When the priest splits up the two verses of the text the woman is made to part her thighs; as the two verses are completed, the sacrificer effects penetration; the syllables of the succeeding verses are then pronounced slowly and separately while the man activates his hips; and when the priest's recitation becomes inaudible the man emits his seed.

The *Shatapatha Brahmana*, another ancient scripture, compares the form of the sacrificial fire altar with the shape of the female, and the fire itself with the testes, saying, 'The joyous embrace of man and woman is the *agnihotra* sacrifice', that is, the ceremony in which the Vedic priest pours an oblation into the sacred fire.

Later hymns and religious texts too, and the Sanskrit and vernacular classics, are replete with passages of similar import, some bordering at times on pornographic writing. India's greatest classical dramatist Kalidasa (fl. A.D. 540) described the loves of Shiva and Parvati with such lubricity that the divine pair are said to have put a curse on him. Indian poetry and song dwell lingeringly and with gusto on the erotic passion of various divine lovers. The *Bhagavata Purana* describes in detail the god Krishna 'making butter with his milkmaids'.

A similar licence is seen in Indian temple sculpture, not only of the Hindus, but of the Buddhists and the otherwise puritanical Jains as well. The sculptures of Puri, Khajuraho and Konarak ('the Black Pagoda') are well known, but hundreds of lesser known shrines throughout the length and breadth of India reflect the same predilection for portraying erotic figures, which fill every available space. Many Indians have expressed their indignation at the representations that decorate the so-called sacred shrines. One eminent Hindu, Purshottamdas Tandon denied that they were in the true Hindu tradition, and has proposed that they should be destroyed.

In these sculptures we find instances of exhibitionism run wild; men with enormous erect penis, and women with vulva cavernous and gaping; men and women in autoerotic scenes; male and female homosexuality; the two sexes in oral-genital congress; promiscuous group sexuality, including cunnilingus, fellatio and anal coitus; men mating with animals; women coupling with the horse, donkey, deer, dog, boar (Desai, 1975). Where male and female figures are not explicitly shown, various symbolic forms of wide ranging significance are substituted: the swastika, to represent the cosmos; the wheel, symbol of the sun's disk; footprints, representing the 'presence' of the deity; the egg, symbol of fertility; also various kinds of geometrical shapes. But above all, those symbols are ubiquitous that have a more direct sexual significance, and of these, the linga (phallus) and the yoni (vulva), separately or in union, are the most common, representing the procreative powers of Shiva and Shakti.

The *Mahabharata* declares that everything in creation bears the signature of the linga and the yoni. It is repeatedly pointed out that pleasure dwells in these organs, which must be used in order to discover and experience the ultimate principles of the universe. They sanctify the worshipper, endowing him with some of their transcendent qualities.

Phallus

The phallus *(linga)* is regarded as the visible symbol of the creator, and it is essential therefore that one recognize its divine nature. The *Shiva Purana* says, 'He who spends his life without honouring the phallus is verily unfortunate, sinful and ill-fated'. Legend relates how the youth Chanda hacked off his father's leg with an axe because the old man had contemptuously kicked a linga image. So pleased was the god Shiva with the lad's devotion that he personally visited the household and garlanded the boy.

According to the *Mahanirvana Tantra* the man who sets up the phallic emblem of Shiva acquires ten million times the merit that is acquired by giving away many acres of land filled with gold, or by digging wells in a waterless country, or by helping the poor and distressed (Woodroffe, 1972, p.334). The mere sight of a linga properly set up and duly consecrated, declares another text, absolves one from all sin, 'even if one has killed a thousand brahmins and ten thousand cows'.

The phallus is worshipped in millions of temples and sacred enclosures throughout India, some of massive proportions, and some of miniature size. Some temples contain a single monolithic representation, and some over a hundred. There are enormous lingas with as many as a thousand lesser lingas engraved on them. Many important pilgrimage centres are famous linga shrines (Walker, 1968, I, p.596).

Where a duly consecrated linga of stone is not available for
worship, substitutes may be used, and these carry, though in
somewhat lesser measure, the merit of the larger idol. Thus, in
the absence of a proper linga a temporary linga can be set up.
This should be made from a mixture of cowdung, butter,
sandalwood paste, grass, flour, and jaggery, to the accompaniment of mantras. Vatsyayana (fl. A.D. 450), the famous Hindu writer on erotics,
records that in the Hindu harems where several women had to
share one husband, they satisfied their sexual desires mutually,
or by recourse to an artificial penis *(apadravya)*. Other works on
erotics relate how such husband-substitutes were anointed and
worshipped before use, and were passed around the harem.
Artificial phalli were also popular outside harems, and these too
received worship.

The living phallus of a holy man is sometimes similarly
revered, especially by women desirous of bearing children, who
render osculatory homage to the member of the holy one to
make themselves fertile. Goldberg speaks of the priests of
Kanara who at certain times used to go naked down the streets
ringing a bell, so that women could perform the sacred duty of
kissing the organ.

Linga symbols include: the thunderbolt *(vajra)*; the rod
(danda); the spear *(shula)*; the fish; the upreared serpent, one of
the most ancient and powerful of phallic symbols; the pillar; the
upward-pointing triangle; any natural object with a phallic
shape.

Vulva

Like the linga, the vulva *(yoni)* is widely depicted and described
in tantrik art and literature. The 'cleft' or 'fissure' of the yoni is
regarded as the dispenser of *bhaga*, 'good luck', a word also used
as a synonym for yoni. From the word bhaga comes the title
Bhagwan, 'god', and *bhagat*, 'devotee'.

The vulva is the 'triangle' of origination'. The *Hevajra Tantra*
says, 'Concentrate upon the triangle of origination in the midst
of space'. Most tantrik sects believe that a man can attain the
highest bliss 'by meditating on the soul seated in the female
organ'. In Buddhist tantrik sects paradise or Sukhavati is likened
to the yoni, and many Vajrayana texts declare unequivocally

that 'Buddhahood lies in the vagina' (Sierksma, 1966, p.52). The yoni is a talisman, bestowing success and victory. Shiva conquered death because he meditated on the life-giving yoni; the god-hero Rama defeated the ten-headed Ravana because he worshipped the yoni of his wife Sita; the five great epic heroes of the *Mahabharata*, the Pandavas, were victorious in battle because they put their trust in the propitious yoni of their common wife, Draupadi (Schoterman, 1980, p.25).

In the *Yoni Tantra*, the yoni is subdivided into ten parts: hair-pit, field, edge, arch, girdle, nodule, cleft, wheel, throne, root, each part being associated with an aspect of the goddess. The yoni is an emblem of the ultimate, the custodian of the great secrets, displaying in its shape the enigmatic *shunya*, 'zero', an emptiness in which all things are contained. In Sanskrit and vernacular writings, the yoni is extolled as a sacred area, a soft pad of pleasure, a zone of felicity, an occult region opening into the *axis mundi*, the crosspoint of the universe and a gateway to the cosmic mysteries.

Tantrik temples are often dedicated to the yoni, and an important part of each tantrik's duties is vulva worship *(yoni puja)*, or the vulva rite *(bhaga yaja)*, in which the vulva of a living woman, or a stone, wooden or pictorial representation is adored, as a symbol of the goddess. Occasionally the goddess herself is sculpted, lying on her back, legs outspread, the whole figure distorted, obscured and foreshortened, so that the vulva may be prominently displayed for ritual worship. Or else the goddess may be shown standing upright, feet apart, while a worshipper of diminutive size kneels beneath her arched legs looking upward into her yoni.

Yoni motifs are frequently drawn in tantrik mandalas and on other objects used in daily life. Its chief symbols are the following: all shells, especially the conch and the cowrie; all flowers, especially the lotus; the circle; the downward-pointing triangle; the coiled snake, which represents the serpentine energy within the female; any natural object of vulvate shape. All ring-stones, or any small stones with a natural perforation are regarded as yoni-stones; they are particularly lucky if they fit the organ of the finder, for he then consecrates the stone and wears it, securing it with a piece of string.

Chakrapuja

The central rite of sexualized tantra is one of congregational worship, in which a group of male and female tantriks, between eight and forty-eight in number, meet at night to participate in a ceremony known as *chakrapuja*, 'circle worship', so called because the celebrants sit side by side in a circle.

The venue may be a remote shrine, an empty house, or the private residence of some wealthy patron, but always in some place hidden from the eyes of outsiders. The rite is still performed in Rajasthan, Bengal, Orissa and other places in India.

Notice of the date, time and place of the ceremony is given secretly to the worshippers about ten days in advance. As sexual intercourse is the climax of the proceedings, and the participants must show no evidence of impotence or frigidity, it is essential that they should be in readiness when the moment arrives. Some prepare themselves by a week's indulgence in highly seasoned foods and meats, as well as aphrodisiacs and erethitic potions, and by refraining from any form of sexual activity. The day preceding the rite is to be observed as a day of total abstinence.

After entering the ritual chamber the participants are offered cannabis or some other aphrodisiac drug, usually made up into small pills prepared with molasses. This is euphemistically called *vijaya*, 'victory-giving'.

In chakrapuja no one has any claim on any woman, and personal preference is not allowed to decide the selection of the partner. Many methods have therefore been devised to ensure that the partners pair not by choice but by chance. One method is called the 'bodice-way' *(choli-marg)*. Each woman entering the sanctuary casts off her bodice or blouse *(choli* or *kanchuli)* into a receptacle, and from this receptacle each man picks at random one of the bodices, and must take as his partner for the occasion the woman to whom it belongs, be that woman his wife, another's wife, his own sister, daughter or mother.

The members sit in a circle on the floor, the sexes alternating, each man's partner sitting on his left. In the middle of the circle is a nude young girl representing the goddess, accompanied by the chief priest, who is the officiating hierophant at the ceremony.

The girl may be seated on a low altar, with legs spread wide apart to display the hallowed symbol of adoration, the yoni, which, like the yonis of all the women present, must be unshaven. Or she may lie spread-eagled on the floor in the pentacle position, her head and outstretched arms and legs forming the five points of a star. She is sprinkled with wine and rendered sacred by the rite of applying *(nyasa)*, the priest ritually implanting upon her limbs the power of the goddess. This he does by lightly touching her forehead, eyes, nostrils, nose, ear lobes, throat, breasts, arms, hands, navel, thighs, knees and feet, with his hands, while intoning appropriate mantras.

Special homage is paid to the yoni, which the priest touches with his lips and anoints with sandalwood paste, and to which he symbolically offers libations from a ritual yoni-shaped vessel called the *argha*. The girl is thus transfigured into Shakti and becomes the deity incarnate. She is adored and worshipped like a goddess and treated as one. The whole congregation now forms a living mandala within the ritual chamber.

If the girl is a virgin an act of ritual defloration takes place. In any case the priest has intercourse with her, and the expended semen is stored in a special receptacle. Colaabavala says, 'Potions containing the semen of an already enlightened guru may have to be drunk in the ceremony' (1980, p.14).

There follows the ritual of communal participation in chakrapuja. The *Kamakhya Tantra* reads, 'The true devotee should worship the Mother of the Universe with liquor, meat, fish, cereal and copulation with women', and this the celebrants proceed to do. In Sanskrit the names of these five elements all begin with the letter *ma*, and for this reason they are known as the five *makara*, or five *ma*-made things, namely: *madya* or wine; *mamsa*, flesh; *matsya*, fish; *mudra*, cereal wafer; and *maithuna*, sexual union.

In the feasting and drinking that follow the men are served by the women, and in the course of this sybaritic revel the women wear bells around their hips and ankles and little else, the metallic tintinnabulation serving to augment both the divine and erotic passions. This 'long-drawn Eucharist' (Rawson, 1973, p.24) lasts for hours, until all concerned are in a state of great sexual tension. They are now ready for the fifth and final element, that of maithuna.

It should be noted that the five traditional elements of the chakrapuja rite are not accepted in their literal sense by all tantriks, who sometimes use substitutes *(pratinidhi)* in their place. The more conservative prefer to give an innocuous and more acceptable interpretation to them; the radically-minded give a more unorthodox listing. Below are a few examples.

Thus, instead of wine, flesh, fish, cereal and coition, some use coconut juice, cheese, ginger, rice and honey. Those who prefer a contemplative interpretation substitute: composing the mind, inbreathing, outbreathing, holding in the breath, meditation. Another alternative: stillness, silence, concentration, inter-weaving of the fingers, recitation of the mantra Om. Or, rather less acceptably: concentration on the anus, testes, vagina, clitoris, phallus. One unorthodox sect makes the following substitution with five words also beginning with the letter *ma*, namely: *meha* (or *mutra*), urine; *mamsa*, human flesh; *mala*, excrement; *medha*, juice, that is, blood; and *mehana*, penis, that is, semen.

Coition

Sexual union or *maithuna* is that act in which a man and woman come together for the mingling of their bodies, the exchange of their fluids, and the mutual recharging of their energy. In what is known as closed maithuna, already mentioned, the man has intercourse without reaching climax. In open maithuna, considered here, the man reaches orgasm in the course of the act. In some tantrik circles maithuna is allowed with more than one partner.

The operation preceding maithuna is mudra. As already explained, the term mudra signifies not only cereal, but also the female partner, as well as the posture adopted during inter-course. In the view of some tantrik scholars, during the mudra phase, each *sadhaka* or aspirant should place his allotted shakti on his left thigh and should honour her yoni. Chakraberty describes the mudra phase as 'excitation of the clitoris by the raised forefinger, the other fingers being closed' (1945, p.303). When she is sufficiently aroused he effects penetration, reciting the prescribed mantras.

In tantrik maithuna, the man and woman adopt different postures in order to draw down and concentrate cosmic potencies, and interior acts of various kinds are performed while both remain perfectly still in their prescribed copulatory asanas. The tantrik emblem of the conjoined couple is the snake coiled around an upright stone. One text states that maximum benefit can be gained if the principal devotee lets a woman fellate him, and a pupil who wishes to share the experience 'can do so by pushing a finger up the worshipper's anus' (Menen, 1974, p.92).

According to the *Vamamarga*, at the moment of ejaculation the tantrik repeats a formula offering his semen to the deities: 'Om. With light and ether in my two fists [testes], I the exulting one offer this oblation lovingly into the fire of the womb. Svaha.' After the act the linga and yoni are laved in water, the water offered to the goddess, and then mixed with wine and drunk by the sadhaka to ensure virility.

The union of the male and female bodies gives the embracing couple the acme of pleasure, the process of satisfying their mutual desires affords the highest state of physical enjoyment. But maithuna is not to be performed merely for the acute physical sensations it provides.

The world attains a state of continuous creation when the yoni receives the infusion of the male seed in sexual delight, but again, maithuna must not be considered in terms of progeny.

In Tibetan psychology, certain xenophrenic, 'other-minded' or trance-like states, are said to be achieved in the moments immediately preceding such conditions as yawning, falling asleep, unconsciousness, death, and orgasm. But again, coition should not be used as a means for experiencing such states.

Guenther writes, 'What on the biological level is represented as sexual intercourse is on the mental level the union or fusion of consciousness with the unconscious (1969, p.47). But again, the alteration of consciousness is not the objective of maithuna.

The tantrik ideal is to transcend sex and to raise maithuna to a spiritual plane. In different texts the state of spiritualized maithuna is called by various names suggestive of ecstasy, mystical union and salvation. The phenomenal world is transcended, dualities abolished, egoness lost, and the two polar opposites fuse into a state of intimate and blissful oneness. It is an experience of the soul's extinction in God, and a foretaste of the divine.

Woman

In Hindu mythology Shiva and Shakti stand for the two
complementary forces pervading the cosmos. Shiva provides
the constituent elements making up its fabric, but he is the
subordinate of the two, for it is Shakti alone who underlies all
manifestation, charges the universe with the potencies inherent
in it, and energizes the whole cosmic process. According to a
tantrik saying, 'Shiva without Shakti is a corpse'. Tantrism is
known by the alternative name of Shaktism, the Tantras are
referred to as Shakta writings, and tantrik cults are often called
Shakta cults.

Woman, as the living embodiment of Shakti, shares in the
creative principle, and is essential to Tantrism in every one of its
aspects. She is treated on terms of complete equality with men,
and in many rites is assigned a superior status. Woman provides
an element that nothing else can give a man, for she represents
the opposite *par excellence*, the contrasting and vitalizing component that brings a vision of the goddess and of the absolute.

The *Guhya-samaja Tantra* declares that salvation does not
depend on abstinence, and each of the five wisdom-manifestations
of Buddha is associated with a female partner. So without a
female partner for the sublimation of sexual rites salvation is
impossible. Women are to be enjoyed as part of the worship of
Buddha. 'Woman', goes a tantrik saying, 'is my highest religion.
She is the highest object of my devotions. She is my heaven.' In
one text Buddha says, 'Women are deities. Women are life.
Women are adornment. Be ever among women in your thoughts'
(Cakravarti, 1963, p.96).

In texts such as the *Tara Tantra* and the *Rudra Yamala*, it is
related that the great sage Vasishtha practised austerities and
yoga for many years, but was unable to obtain any powers
(siddhis), and was told to go to Maha-china (Tibet or China).
There he found Buddhists trained in the drinking of blood and
other such reprehensible rites, and indulging in wine and meat
in the company of a host of nude females. Later he beheld
Buddha himself surrounded by beautiful women in erotic
ecstasy. Vasishtha expressed great indignation and horror at
these practices, but a voice from heaven bade him follow the
'Chinese way', and Buddha endorsed this view. Thenceforth
Vasishtha took to eating meat, drinking wine and enjoying sex

with women, and became a great yogi (Cakravarti, 1963, p.96).

Women are the source of fertility and abundance, and are held to be supreme in all ways. They promote auspiciousness, well-being and prosperity; avert bad luck and calamity; and drive away evil spirits. They cause the rain to fall, aid agricultural fruitfulness and give fertility to cattle. They bear children, provide milk, and every month they make an offering of their innermost blood to the great goddess.

· Women are meant both for enjoyment *(bhoga)* and for worship *(puja)*. Hence many rites actually involve woman-worship *(stri-puja)*. As a representative of the goddess the female is spoken of as *shakti*, which means 'power'; she is also *mudra* or 'joy-giving'; and *vidya*, 'wisdom', like Sophia or 'wisdom' of the Gnostics.

That woman is particularly extolled who is of sweet breath and whose vulva is as fragrant as a lotus flower. She should have lotus eyes, full breasts, soft skin, a slender waist, a fine neck, lustrous hair, and a prominent mons veneris. By the sight of such beauty, 'the phallus is enticed into the yoni' (Mookerjee, 1971, p.37). In the words of one tantrik text, the man should 'embrace his female partner, drink from her lips, insert his organ into her vulva, enjoying rich delights, making her thighs shake and her inner parts quiver'.

According to the *Chhandogya Upanishad* a man procreates himself at each intercourse, and the rule is therefore that one should never abstain from any woman. The *Guhya-samaja Tantra* says, 'All women that are in the world the tantrik may enjoy in order to experience the mahamudra'. The *Yoni Tantra* states that the yoni of any woman between the ages of twelve and sixty will do, if she is 'experienced or wanton'.

But for the purpose of tantrik sex rites, women are graded according to their ritual merit, each grade more unorthodox than the preceding, each step in the direction of unorthodoxy being regarded as so much more meritorious and pointing the way to a higher experience of bliss and consequent spiritual benefits. Thus the partner may be, in rising order of preference: one's own wife; a woman of lower caste, especially an outcaste; a prostitute, dancing girl or actress; a woman of higher caste, especially a brahmin; a virgin; another man's wife; one's own sister, daughter, mother; a demoness or other being of the elemental, etheric or astral planes.

Adultery and Incest
In all parts of the world social attitudes towards family relation-
ships have varied from age to age. In ancient India both adultery
and incest were often lightly treated. The Vedic sage Yajnavalkya,
who wrote a famous legal code, declared that the transgressions
of a married woman, unless they bore fruit, were washed away by
her next menstrual flow. The god Krishna was said to have been
particularly well disposed to women who left their husbands to
follow him, and one of his favourite mistresses, Radha, was the
wife of a cowherd. Krishna also disported himself sexually with
the wives of the brahmins of Mathura.

In the tantrik view normal marital relations with one's own
wife are devoid of merit. Married love lacks intensity, and the
relationship between husband and wife soon becomes dutiful,
conventional and neutral, continued only to ease a sensual ache
or for the sake of progeny. It lacks the keen edge of passion. It is
not wanton, abandoned or free, and therefore can never lead to
the kind of ecstatic transport sought by the tantrik.

One way of remedying this situation is to seek coitus with the
wife of someone else, especially if she is newly wed. For his part
the tantrik must be prepared to allow his wife to be used in the
same way by others. He is expressly enjoined not to be jealous or
object if another desires to enjoy his wife.

Incestuous congress is a further stepping stone on the
upward grade to emancipation and enlightenment. And this
too, it would seem, has ancient authority. Dr S. C. Sarkar thinks
that the *Rig-Veda* furnishes rishi sanction for incestuous ties
between a man and his sister, or even mother, and certain early
Vedic rites involved the union of a man with his own sister or
mother. Incestuous relations were of course customary in many
ancient civilizations.

The tantriks too advocate incest with one's near female
relatives. Special honour accrues to him whose linga enters into
his own 'mother's vulva' *(matri-yoni)*, since this completes a cycle
broken at birth. A verse in the *Anangavajra* reads, 'The adept who
has sexual intercourse with his mother, his sister, his daughter,
his niece, will easily succeed in his striving for the ultimate goal'
(Guenther, 1969, p.118), a point also repeated in the *Guhya-*

samaja Tantra, which says that such an adept will advance towards 'the highest perfection'.

Orthodox Hindus, with obvious justification, have condemned such practices outright. Swami Dayananda (d. 1883) founder of the influential Arya Samaj sect wrote after studying tantrik philosophy, 'My astonishment knew no bounds when I read with my own eyes in tantrik books of the sexual intercourse of mother and son, of the worship of naked women, of the taking of wine and drugs, and that salvation was expected through all this'.

Ramakrishna (d. 1886) the modern Indian saint, had been introduced to tantrik magical practices and yogic techniques by a mendicant nun, and later stated that some of the methods were so dangerous that they could cause a devotee to sink into utter moral degradation.

The Virgin
Another category of female with whom the tantrik sought to have intercourse was the virgin, although she was taboo for this purpose in the usual social situation. Again, as in many other early cultures, the virgin was assigned a special place in Hinduism and was thought to possess a special power.

On first contact with the 'male rod' as it penetrated her, a virgin's secret parts were believed to flash forth a devastating aura that could bring blight to the man, so that ill luck would follow him thereafter. If by some chance he were spared these calamities in this world, he would receive his deserts in more terrible form in the next world. A man is believed to be particularly prone to injury from this poisonous flash because the excitement of the sexual act renders him defenceless against its psychic impact.

The deities of course were immune to its malefic influence and were in no danger of contamination from sexual contact with virgins, but even so few of them cared to have encounters with virgins. The exception was the god Krishna who consorted freely with the milkmaids who tended the cows of Vrindavana, and whom he is supposed to have seduced in their thousands, having first maddened them with the music of his flute.

There were also certain classes of people who were regarded as endowed with the power to withstand the danger attendant

on the act of defloration. Kings, symbolizing the majesty and
might of the realm, were able to neutralize the scathing shock
while plucking the maiden flower. By the sacred nature of their
calling priests too were immune to the contaminating flash.
Similarly, the marriage ceremony, duly performed before the
sacred altar and consecrated by a priest, inoculates the lawful
bridegroom against its harmful effects, so a bridegroom has no
cause to fear having intercourse with his virgin bride.

The ancient Vedic rishi Shvetaketu declared that the defloration of virgins outside marriage brought disaster to the
nation. Prosperous kingdoms came to their end not because
they were corrupted by luxury, but because disregard for the
sanctity of the virgin knot removed the protective barriers
against the invasion of destructive forces from the unseen
world. For this reason he ordained that promiscuity involving
virgins be everlastingly unthinkable.

The left-hand cults were no less aware of the hazards
surrounding unlawful sexual intercourse with virgins, and some
Tantras warn against such action, as 'there is the loss of
supernatural powers every time' (Schoterman, 1980, p.18).
Tantriks knew well that hymenal blood brought psychic contamination, and so regarded the act as extremely injurious.

Tantrik adepts therefore evolved a protective ritual by means
of which they were able to deflect the danger towards the
innocent girl herself and utilize for magical purposes the
residual gynergy released during her defloration. From medieval
times tantrik retreats were noted as hotbeds of sex practices
involving virgins. According to a Hindu historian, 'even innocent
maidens visiting monasteries were seduced to surrender their
chastity to the monks to help the latter attain Realization'
(Jindal, 1955, p.33).

The texts prescribe that the girl chosen for defloration
should have attained puberty and should be just blossoming
into womanhood, but for the purpose of attaining perfection
the tantrik may have intercourse with a girl who had not yet
started menstruating. In the rite of 'virgin-worship' *(kumari-
puja)*, a girl is selected and trained for initiation, and innocent of
her impending fate is brought before the altar and worshipped
in the nude, and then deflowered by a guru or chela. Deprived of
her virgin power in this manner, she is thereafter of no more use

to the tantrik than the husk of a shelled peanut.

Outcastes and Harlots

In Tantrism the woman who is the object of worship or intercourse is not necessarily selected for her superficial attributes of social or sexual desirability. There is, says the tantrik, no difference between Draupadi (a voluptuous heroine of the *Mahabharata* epic) and a *dombi* (a low-caste untouchable woman). In the *Jnana-siddhi* it is stated that the tantrik who has intercourse with a *dombi* or any woman who comes from a low-caste family attains perfection. Union with such a woman will help him to shatter the trammels of caste and of social convention.

Women of the lowest classes, outcastes and untouchables, and females of depraved character and debauched life, such as 'actresses, dancers and singers, and other public women who exposed their persons', were all regarded as possessing special virtues in this respect, and were often recruited to serve as shaktis and sexual partners in various tantrik rites.

For the same reason the services of the prostitute were eagerly sought. She was regarded as having overcome the normal woman's diffidence about sleeping around. Her body and especially her vagina had been in sensuous contact with numberless men. Such a woman's body, mind and spirit were ready for tantrik use. The semen of a man who has been continent for some weeks, when emitted into the yoni of a prostitute, becomes very potent and can be made to yield magical results.

Closely associated with the kind of occult operations pursued by the tantrik were the women who served in religious shrines. These women, known as *devadasis*, 'servants of the gods', were temple prostitutes. As such they combined two qualities beloved by the tantrik: religion and sexuality.

In the highest grades of Tantrism a woman is picked not only for her evil reputation but also for her lack of aesthetic appeal. The chief female hierophants among the tantriks were the *dakinis* (see below), who were often old crones of revolting ugliness. There is no room in Tantrism for the man who cannot overcome his personal and acquired preferences. Beauty is a snare and an impediment, and the further a woman is removed from such deceptive enticements the better, for then the full

abstract potency of the Female can be brought into operation in
its pure and unadulterated state.

Ugly, old and depraved women are often the favoured choice
in the highest tantrik rites, as they are the living embodiment of
the Vulva, transcending all considerations of beauty, youthfulness, wealth, virtue and social status.

Congressus Subtilis

Among the last phases of the tantrik's progress is sexual union
on the astral plane, when he invokes elemental spirits, fiendesses,
and the spirits of the dead, and has intercourse with them. In one
supreme exercise of his adepthood he brings consternation to
heaven by uniting with the goddesses in the highest spheres. In
the *Guhya-samaja Tantra* Buddha himself is portrayed in acts of
continuous venery with angelic beings, and in other tantrik
texts such acts are held up for emulation, although admittedly a
deeper symbolic interpretation has been put forward in mitigation
of this aspect of Tantrism.

This form of phallic sorcery is said to be known only to a few
great adepts. Little is committed to writing lest its incorrect
practice break the continuum of the universe and bring on the
final chaos.

Buddhists believe that there are six orders of existence, four
of them inhabiting the spiritual, astral, etheric and elemental
planes, and invisible to us, the fifth being men, and the sixth
animals. It is possible, the claim is, to invoke the beings of these
other dimensions, and to communicate and have congress with
them. Such subtle congress may take place between a male
human being and a female elemental called a succubus, or
between a woman and a male elemental or incubus.

Sir John Woodroffe speaks of tantrik adepts who by mastering
the art of *prayoga* acquire the magical power of invoking female
elementals, and drawing on their 'female energy' *(nayika siddhi)*
during intercourse with them.

Rivière in *Tantrik Yoga* says that he personally knew 'the
absolutely depraved and abnormal sexual appetites of these
false yogis', who by using certain occult methods were able to
visualize and animate and give a kind of materiality to female
entities known as succubi. It is also thought possible for an
adept in his astral body to visit a sleeping person and have

congress either with that person's physical or astral body.

The ultimate goal of every tantrik sorcerer is union with the awesome *dakini*, the elemental embodiment of supernatural knowledge and ability. The five chief dakinis are revered as the consorts of the *dakas*, the terror deities of the tantrik pantheon; and as the 'five immortal sisters' they are known to the oldest esoteric traditions of China, Mongolia, Tibet and India. In Hinduism the dakini is described as belonging to the retinue of the goddess Kali. In Tibetan occultism she is known as the 'sky-going woman' *(kha-do-ma)*, or female who travels in the void. These primeval hags of preternatural power dwell in invisible palaces made of bones and skins that are raised over cemeteries and other dread places.

The dakini is of protean form and function. In varying contexts she is demoness, succubus, sorceress, prostitute, initiatrix and vampire. She stays near the dying to carry off their last breath, and the death rites, especially of the Tibetans, are partly designed to stave off their astral attacks. Dakinis frequently figure in the lives of siddhas and adepts of the left hand, and in popular Tantrism the female leader of a left-hand coven is referred to as a dakini.

Dakinis are hostile to the ordinary run of human beings, and to those rash individuals who seek their knowledge without due preparation they like to appear in voluptuous guise, and intercourse with them gives indescribable pleasure. But the experience may well prove disastrous, for with their long pendulous labia they engulf a man's penis and 'suck his testicles dry'.

In their real and undisguised form they are creatures of unbelievable ugliness, with long emaciated breasts and huge sex organs of offensive odour. Their mouths drip with blood and they smell of carrion flesh. Often they will yield their secrets only after being violently raped.

According to tradition, the dakini who initiated the Tibetan teacher Tilopa (c. A.D. 960) bore on her person the 'eighteen marks of ugliness'. The one who gave secret instruction to Tilopa's pupil Naropa (d. 1039) was described as 'an ugly, leprous old crone' of extreme repulsiveness. Naropa's pupil Marpa (d. 1096) himself received initiation from a foul-smelling 'funeral-place dakini' (see Hoffmann, 1961).

These creatures are guardians of the blackest mysteries, who initiate specially endowed persons into the terrifying rites of necrosexuality.

4.

TANTRA AND DEATH

Violence

As already indicated Tantrism opposes the traditional attitudes to religion, morality and sexual and family life. Underlying its more extreme aspects is the encouragement of those emotions of violence and aggression that have been condemned in other faiths as deadly sins.

Speaking of such passions as greed, anger and hatred, a modern tantrik teacher, Bhagwan Shree Rajneesh says, 'Take them as divine gifts and approach them with a grateful heart' (1976, p.35).

The propagation of such a creed, so easily open to mis-understanding, if extended into the wider area of social life can lead to disastrous consequences. In the more sinister tantrik sects these hostile emotions are sedulously cultivated, and specific instruction imparted to increase their virulence and finally give vent to them in deliberate animosity and lawless conduct.

As a cult obligation, followers are enjoined to carry out acts of a progressively more and more anti-social nature; to tell lies in preference to the truth, to steal what belongs to others, to commit robbery and violence, and in the final phase, to commit murder (see Desai, 1975, p.123).

In certain forms of tantrik initiation, the candidate is asked whether, for the sake of the goddess, he would be prepared to kill anyone, even members of his own family: father, wife, child (Colaabavala, 1980, p.28). Twenty-one murder rites are known to exist. The *Kaulavali-nirnaya* and related texts give full in-structions on the meditation, mantras and yantras of these cults.

Killing, it is believed, gives one a dark aura of destructive energy. Soldiers, butchers, executioners, assassins, are said to have great occult power, even when they are unaware of it, and are unable to use it.

Cruelty and bloodshed have characterized the activities of a number of tantrik sects, old and new. The Kapalikas and cults related to them, have performed human sacrifices and ritual murder as a form of daring *(bala)* to please the goddess. Among the many orders of armed ascetics were the Sajjikas, who carried swords and daggers and openly advocated violence as a religious obligation. The infamous Pindaris and Dacoits took drugs and intoxicants and performed blood sacrifices at their ceremonies, before setting forth on their murderous expeditions. Associated with the goddess in her terror aspect of Bhavani, were the Thugs, a secret society of assassins who, to please and propitiate her, waylaid and strangled travellers by slow garrotting. Several groups of religious marauders, for want of any categorizable status, were classed as Criminal Tribes, and had a tradition of cult murder as part of their religion. The Anand Marg sect received notoriety a few years ago when hundreds of skulls were discovered in their cult centres throughout India.

By recourse to black magic, astral influence, and the conjuration of evil powers, tantrik gurus are supposed to be able to gain control over the lives and fortunes of their followers, who in recent times have been represented in all strata of society, including university professors, police officers, lawyers, government functionaries, even ministers of state. Those initiates rash enough to disclose the inner secrets have on occasion been silenced for good,and in some cases apparently their entire families were 'wiped off' (Colaabavala, 1980, p.9).

In the ritual contests between rival magicians, it is understood that the loser will commit suicide. Colaabavala describes some of the more macabre cases. A few years ago an Indian government official and member of a tantrik cult, was forced to burn himself alive by an enemy tantrik, and did so in full public view at a Shiva temple in Ujjain. His wife had died of burn injuries some six months earlier. In 1964, a murder sacrifice lasting some seven weeks was allegedly held at the Durga temple in Mirzapur, Uttar Pradesh, for the purpose of bringing about the death of the then Prime Minister, Pandit Jawaharlal Nehru. By a curious coincidence he died within three months (Pawar, 1981, p.67).

Tantriks are men of strange and malignant force, and it is widely believed in India that it is dangerous to thwart or provoke them, for they are malicious in the extreme. Allegedly they can torment and drive a person mad by projecting into his mind some overwhelming obsession that he is unable to shake off, so that he finally succumbs and commits suicide. They measure the shadow of a victim with a length of string, and then, by knotting that string, 'knot' or block the inner channels of the victim's body. Or they make an effigy of him and nail it down, and so injure some vital organ of the man himself. Their maledictions are supposed to stun, paralyse, cripple, and cause cruel and agonizing death.

Blood Sacrifice

Blood plays an important part in tantrik black magical rites both in India and Tibet. Tibetan manuals on magic give detailed information about the kinds of blood most useful in the different rites. These include: the blood of a black horse, black cat, black dog or raven; the blood of a child who is the fruit of an incestuous union; the blood of a young man killed in a fight or murdered; the menstrual blood of a prostitute; the blood from the head of a lunatic; the blood of a man suffering from a dangerous or contagious disease, especially leprosy. The liquid so used may be further potentized by being mixed with drugs.

Such blood is offered to demons and spirits when calling down evil powers of particular malevolence. It is also smeared on the bodies of those participating in the ceremony, in place of the scented oils and perfumed water that are ordinarily used.

Sometimes blood is obtained from ritual sacrifices, animal or human. Where they can find the opportunity devotees will subject their victims to a lingering death, preferably under prolonged torture, as by this means the flesh, bones and blood are believed to be properly confected.

Ten kinds of animal victims are mentioned in the *Mahanirvana Tantra*, namely: the goat, lamb, deer, buffalo, hog (in Tibet, pig's blood was regarded as very efficacious), porcupine, hare, alligator, tortoise and rhinoceros. A short formula is recited, the sacrificial blade is worshipped, and after dedicating the animal to the goddess it is slain.

Human victims are the most desirable when available, for the

deities joyfully receive oblations of human flesh mixed with
brains, marrow and entrails (Lorenzen, 1972, p.85). In the past
human sacrifice was not uncommon in Tibet, although the
Buddhist lamas protested against it. The blood was drunk and
the skull and skin used for drinking vessels, whips and saddles.
In India sects like the Kapalikas and Kalamukhas were on the
look-out for beautiful young women whom they could offer as a
sacrifice to the fierce goddess Chamunda, another aspect of
Shakti. The Shakta treatise, the *Kalika Purana*, devotes an entire
chapter to animal and human sacrifice. 'By a human sacrifice', it
is said, 'the goddess remains gratified for a thousand years. By
the sacrifice of three men, one hundred thousand years'.

Lord Hastings, governor-general of India put down the
Pindaris in 1818. Lord Bentinck, a later governor-general
undertook extremely drastic measures, amounting almost to
war, against the Thugs and suppressed them by 1861. By the end
of the nineteenth century British law and Hindu reform had
virtually put an end to the practice of human sacrifice, though
cases of such sacrifice continue to be sporadically reported from
Rajasthan, Madya Pradesh, Uttar Pradesh, Bihar and Andhra
Pradesh to this day.

Necrophilia
Many old tantrik temples were built near cremation grounds or
burial sites, or in some desolate spot where a tragic deed like
murder or suicide, or a bloody battle had taken place. The
preferred habitat of Shaivite and Shakta ascetics is a graveyard,
and tantriks who aspire to sinister power make their homes and
choose as their place of meditation, tombs, charnel fields and
funeral sites. Certain sexual rites are best carried out, says
Rawson, with a menstruating woman 'in a cremation ground
among the corpses and flaming pyres' (1973, p.24).

The apparel of the tantrik sorcerer, either normal or ritual,
may be a flayed-off animal or, more rarely, human skin, for a
covering, a cranium top for a head-dress to cover his long
matted hair, a necklace of teeth or bone fragments, a girdle of
snakeskin, iron bracelets and huge ear-rings. He smears his
body with bone-ash or earth scraped off an exhumed corpse.

His food-bowl is a skull, preferably of a brahmin (Desai, 1975,
p.123), his drinking cup the skull of a monkey or other small

animal, and his spoon a raven's beak. The meditation cell of one of the immured Tibetan monks was found on inspection to be hung with human hair, skin, skeletons and bones, which he had apparently collected from a charnel field. A great number of dried female breasts were hanging on a line, and his food bowl consisted of the dried and cured skin of a woman's breast (Sierksma, 1966, p.189).

The birds and animals with which the tantrik sadhu is popularly associated, and whose flesh, fat and bones he uses for his operations, are the tiger, the jackal, the bat, rat, snake and mad dog, the screech owl, the raven, the crow, vulture and other carrion birds of ill omen.

His implements are the magic rod, the three-pronged stick, the flaying knife and the ritual dagger of human bone (Tibetan, *phurba*). His musical instruments may include a forearm bone for a trumpet, an eerie demon-evoking horn (Tibetan, *kangling*), made of a human femur, a drum made of human skin drawn over a human skull, a small double-drum, and a bell with a thin ghostly tinkle.

The mantras are funeral prayers, garbled and perverted, and terrifying conjurations, repeated over and over again in some now unknown and probably long-forgotten tongue. They are addressed to demons and ghouls. The mandalas themselves have an irregular geometry, outlined with dust from a crossroads or cemetery, or drawn on the back or breast of a corpse or on the ground around it. Sometimes the mandala is danced out, to the accompaniment of a mantra, in a series of strange gyrations performed by the tantrik as he hops about on one foot, leaps into the air, and suddenly steps sideways, weaving, as it were, a mandala in three dimensions.

The tantrik sorcerer has his own asanas or yogic postures of peculiar contortion, which he assumes in meditation and for calling down and controlling spirits. Thus in the skull seat *(munda-asana)* he sits with a skull pressed against his genitals. In the corpse seat *(shava-asana)* he lies prostrate or squats upon a rotting corpse. In the funeral-pyre seat *(chit-asana)* he sits on the site of a funeral pyre.

He makes ritual use of gruesome relics of the dead, such as charred bones, eyeballs, testicles, tongues, as well as the marrow, fat and excrement from a corpse. He will use the soiled linen of an untouchable woman, the menstrual pad of a prostitute, the shroud taken off a corpse, the discarded rag of a leper, the sputum of a consumptive, the semen of an epileptic, and the vomit of an old man poisoned with hemp seeds.

Man's brain is regarded as one of the most important magical areas, and because the skull is in constant touch with it, the skull is treated as a major reservoir of force. The Kapalika sect of tantriks are so named from the human skull *(kapala)* which they always carry with them.

The *Goraksha-siddhanta Samgraha* gives the mythological origin of this cult. It relates that the avatars (incarnations) of the god Vishnu despoiled the earth, frightened the animals, oppressed the towns and villages and did other mischief. The god Krishna, himself one of these avatars, likewise became afflicted with evil and adulterous thoughts. To punish this wickedness Shiva came down and cut off the heads of the avatars and carried their skulls about with him, and the Kapalikas continue this practice in commemoration of Shiva's feat. Shiva later restored the skulls.

The best time for the necromantic ceremonies of Tantrism is from midnight to three hours past midnight, preferably during the dark fortnight of the lunar month, that is, when the moon is waning. The three moonless nights preceding the new moon are the most favoured. According to the *Yoni Tantra*, if a person performs the vulva-rite during the eclipse of the sun or moon he will be free forever, and never be reincarnated on earth again.

Confrontation with death, putrefaction and horror in all its harshness is an essential experience in the tantrik's training. The rites must be performed in solitude, and sometimes involve an elaborate liturgy and this must be learnt by heart. Long preparation, full concentration, supernormal endurance and an inflexible will are demanded of him. The tantrik must succeed, for failure may mean his own death.

Tantriks believe that in order to advance one must be able to override the inherited revulsion arising from intimate contact with a corpse *(shava)*. The horror and sense of guilt can drive the unprepared novice over the brink. Practitioners have been known to lose their reason, to die of fright, to commit suicide.

What is called the corpse-way *(shava-vada)* involves close contact with cadavers, and with the necromantic objects mentioned above, which are meditated upon and constitute the material of cult practice. Tantriks touch, wash and clothe corpses and otherwise assist in the disposal of bodies, and this, it is believed, puts terrifying potentialities within their grasp.

There are many variants of a ceremonial known by the generic term 'black ritual' *(nila-sadhana)*, which is counted among the most secret and perilous 'short paths' to occult power. In one such rite, called *chod*, from the Tibetan word for 'cutting', the practitioner goes at dead of night to a graveyard or cremation ground and invites the spirits to a feast. He then performs his own funeral obsequies, and symbolically sacrifices himself, offering up his body for the delectation of the assembled spirit vampires.

When the spectral guests have departed after their repast, the tantrik is left alone, his bones scattered, the earth dark with his blood, the stench of his own raw flesh in his nostrils. Slowly he reassembles his scattered limbs and organs and returns to wholeness.

Tantriks who have performed the chod rite declare that spirits actually come and feed upon their body, and that they can hear the crunching of bones and the sounds of noisy mastication. They confirm that they actually experience the full agony of their dismemberment. Tantrik teachers say that in this mystic drama the elementals who gather round for the gory meal are creations actualized out of the practitioner's own mind by the force of his highly-charged visualization.

In another version of the black ritual known in Tibetan as *ro-langs*, 'corpse-raising', the tantrik repairs to a solitary place at a time astrologically appropriate, sits astride a male corpse, and by occult means and the recitation of mantras, allegedly animates it by inviting evil spirits and the undead to possess it. He may then command it to answer questions; or behead it, or cut out its tongue or other portion of the 'enlivened' body, for divination or other magical purpose. The corpse may be made to ejaculate and its semen collected and used. Variations of these necromantic themes are too numerous and revolting to quote.

Some of the extreme left-hand sects of India consume scatological substances: dung, urine, blood, bile and semen, as well as the flesh of dogs and other tabooed animals, with the same relish as if it were food offered to the gods. In certain rites the Kapalikas, Aghoris, Shavavadins and related sects, eat the 'great meat' *(maha-mamsa)*, which is human flesh, either cooked or raw, regarding the brain, liver, lungs, bowels and testicles as especially vitalizing. These they obtain from an unburied or exhumed corpse, or a body not wholly consumed in the funeral pyre.

As part of yet another necromantic ritual they will mate with a male or female corpse, since contact of the tantrik's penis with the vulva or anus of the dead is thought to be capable of charging him with supernatural potency. In turn the ejaculated semen of the practitioner is believed to revitalize the corpse and temporarily restore it to life. Tantriks also reputedly buy the bodies of young and beautiful girls, keep the corpse warm for several days on heated bricks, and then have intercourse with it (Colaabavala, 1980, p.60).

The Terror Deities

The gods of the tantrik pantheon are the great terror deities, who are sometimes portrayed in situations of eroticism and in graveyard scenes, characterized by drastic sexuality and aggressiveness. When depicted in paintings they are shown with penis erect, because procreation and death are inextricably linked.

The terror *(bhairav)* element is prominent both in Hindu and Buddhist Tantrism. Its source is Shiva in his aspect of Bhairava, the terrible one, and his consort Shakti in her aspect of Bhairavi, who are imagined as two emaciated figures copulating amid a forest of decaying corpses and dried bones. In their terror aspects the deity and his spouse are described as black-visaged, black-limbed, wrathful and destructive, with ghouls and ogresses for companions. Shiva is king of the vampires *(vetalas)*, Shakti queen of the demonesses *(dakinis)*. Their rites are sombre necromantic mysteries carried out in graveyards, and their canon the unrecorded *Bhairava Tantra*.

Lesser gods include such awe-inspiring beings as Heruka, Kalachakra, Hevajra, Samvara and Mahakala, all blood-drinking terror-beings known as *dakas*, who are conjured up in burial grounds by means of spells and magic mandalas whose designs have to be very carefully learned and meticulously inscribed.

Travellers have often pointed out the strange contrast

between the austere and serene atmosphere of a Tibetan monastery with its gentle and friendly inmates, and the terror aspect of the holiest innermost shrine, dedicated to cruel gods who are presented in frightening attitudes of menace, or as skeletons locked in the *yab-yum*, 'male-female' posture of sexual union. The entrance hall to this inner sanctuary may be decorated with the 'dead and decomposing bodies of animals like wild dogs, yak, snakes and bears' (Rao, 1977, p.20).

In the literary descriptions and in the paintings and sculptures of India and especially Tibet, tantrik deities are invested with all the trappings of fear and dread, as a reminder of the merciless processes of nature. They are surrounded by a circle of fire which rages in their vicinity, making them unapproachable. Black whirlwinds and poisonous vapours sweep across the barren plains where they dwell, bringing pestilence in their wake. There are flashes of lightning, purple in colour, and the air reverberates to the noise of thunder. It is a region both horrible and ferocious. Some of the gods have deformed faces, bloodshot eyes and jutting fangs, and their mouths are contorted in a sneering grimace. Their blood-flecked bodies are covered with human fat and grease stains.

They stand in a plain strewn with the mouldering corpses of toppled kings and dethroned prelates. They wear necklaces of human heads, arms and legs. In their several hands they hold a cranium brimming with steaming blood, a meat cleaver, a copper sword, and other weapons of death. Ravens, screech-owls and other demonic birds fill the air with their evil-portending cries, and over all there hangs a thick mist of blood, fat and pus (Sierksma, 1966, p.26).

In the chapels dedicated to Tibet's terror deities, Giuseppe Tucci says, 'You would think you were looking out over primordial chaos' (1949, I, p.320).

5.

HISTORY OF TANTRISM

The main strands of tantrik thought and practice can be traced back to prehistoric times. Basically these include the worship of the great mother goddess, of the sexual forces, of fertility, and of natural phenomena, such as we find in animism. Some of the symbols used by the modern tantrik, like those of the male and female procreative organs, are similar to those found on the walls of palaeolithic caves (c. 20,000 years ago) from Western Europe to China. It is the persistence of this primitive trait in Tantrism that has prompted scholars to say that the essential elements of the cult are probably older than any of the world's major religions.

An instinctive sense of awe before the forces of nature became associated with a reverence for those who apparently could propitiate and placate these forces by religio-magical practices, and led to the emergence of the shaman, sorcerer and witch-doctor. The shaman has long been held in high popular regard throughout Central Asia for the power he is believed to possess over animals and men, and for the control he exercises over the major events of human experience, birth, copulation and death. He is a man possessing 'prestige', who can create illusions and make people see and imagine things by 'glamour'. It is to be noted that in the West, the terms 'prestige' and 'glamour', like the terms 'fascination' and 'charm' have a witchcraft origin.

Tartary
Scholars have sought some central diffusion area from which the basic notions of shamanism may have spread abroad. Most commonly it is thought to have been located in a semi-legendary region situated somewhere in the depths of Asia

between Afghanistan and China. This vast area extends from the barren Hindu Kush mountains branching westwards from the Himalayas, and stretches northward to Sinkiang and Uighur, and as far east as the plateau of Manchuria. The most favoured location is the territory now covered by the Gobi desert.

This region was the home of early magic, black and white, and was known as Tartary. The name itself is of uncertain origin, and in historical times was frequently confused with the name of the wild and intractable Mongolian tribe known as the Tatars.

In mythology Tartary is the Tartarus of the Greeks, a deep and sunless place beneath Hades, to which the Titans and anti-gods are consigned and punished for their presumption. In occult tradition Tartary is a vague hinterland situated somewhere in Inner Asia, and has long represented the centre of a dangerous maelstrom of black occultism.

Even in historical times it was regarded as the very heart of mysteries. The mystic Emanuel Swedenborg (d. 1772) held that many dark secrets of which we have no inkling 'may peradventure be found in Tartary'. The stygian abyss of Tartary still symbolizes the evil attractions of the occult underworld. Today this mysterious demesne remains one of the least known regions on earth. It is the scene of nature at her most remote, her most serene and also her wildest and stormiest. Once it was the cradle of races now extinct, and of civilizations that survive only in the folk memory of mankind.

From this region comes the tradition, many millenia old, of a powerful kingdom situated on a large island, ringed by snow-capped mountains and dominated by an outstanding peak, the Mount Meru (or Sumeru) of Eastern legend. In her *Secret Doctrine*, Madame Blavatsky (d. 1891) suggests that the wasteland of Tartary was once a great inland sea in which was an island 'inhabited by the last remnant of the Race which preceded ours'. It was, she adds, 'the seat of one of the richest empires the world has ever seen'.

In the centre of the island stood its capital, a splendid city with palaces, temples and colleges of occult learning. There is, at present, no historical evidence for such an empire, only a tradition, widely diffused, but tradition, it must be remembered, plays a very significant part in the occult, even though historians may not set great store by it. To the occultist the hearsay

records preserved in the writings, apocryphal or otherwise, of
Manetho (d. 230 B.C.) on Egyptian history; of Berosus (d. 275
B.C.) on Babylonian history; and of Sanchoniathon (c. 350 B.C.)
on Phoenician history, dating back to periods up to twenty
thousand years ago, are as important as the established histories
pieced together by later archaeologists and historiographers.

The hierophants of many ancient nations knew of the
existence of such an island, the homeland of the Great White
Brotherhood of the modern Theosophists. The early geographers
spoke of the island of Ultima Thule, sometimes said to be
located in the polar north in the country of the Hyperboreans,
and sometimes in the remote east. The Greeks also knew of a
White Island somewhere in the north-east. Achilles the Greek
hero, restored to life, still lives in this island. The home of the
gods of ancient Sumeria, the fabled land of Dilmun, was
described as a paradise situated in the east, where the sun rises.

The Indian epic, the *Mahabharata*, tells of the inhabitants of
Shveta-dvipa, 'white island', on the northern shores of the
Ocean of Milk. In the seventh century the Viking expeditions
returned home with legends of a land called Hvetramannland,
the country of the white men. Russian folklore, too, tells of the
land of Belovodye, or white waters, somewhere in Tartary or
Mongolia. It has some nebulous connection with Grad Kitezh, a
mysterious invisible city of the holy ones. Perhaps these old
traditions formed the basis of modern idyllic paradises, such as
those described in the *Utopia* (1516) of Thomas More, the *City of
the Sun* (1623) of Thomas Campanella, and the *New Atlantis*
(1624) of Francis Bacon.

In this island kingdom, as in Atlantis, two opposing factions
struggled for supremacy. Their names were Agharti and
Shambhala. Agharti, also sometimes known as the White
Shambhala, was the virtuous faction of the right-hand path,
whose meditations were of quiet contemplation. Ranged against
them were the forces of Shambhala, preaching a doctrine of
violence and power. Their magicians were adepts in sorcery and
the diabolic arts, and Shambhala was the source of the left-hand
tradition and black magic.

Some thirty or forty centuries ago, a great conflict took place.
The two forces clashed and there followed a catastrophic war,
'possibly of an atomic nature', according to one modern writer.

The Gobi was transformed into a howling desert, whose sands
are still blown about by terrifying gales. As the island continents
of Atlantis in the Western ocean, of Lemuria in the Indian
Ocean, and of Mu in the Pacific, all vanished under the waves, so
this civilization perished beneath the sands because of its
iniquity. An interconnection between the great centres of left-
hand occultism in the prehistoric past was suggested by the
theosophist Guy de Purucker, who describes the Tantras as
'heirlooms handed down from originally debased or degenerate
Atlantean racial offshoots' (Garrison, 1972, p.50).

In some accounts, after the cataclysmic upheaval that brought
the Gobi kingdom to an end, the remnants of Agharti went
underground, and this belief gave rise to the strange tradition of
the Hollow Earth and the wondrous kingdom of Subterra
(Gardner, 1920; Dickhoff, 1965; Bernard, 1963 and 1969).
Writers like Ferdinand Ossendowski speak of Agharti as still
extant (1923, p.303). The wisdom teachings of Agharti made
their contribution to the orthodox religions of the East, like
Zoroastrianism, Vedism, Buddhism and Jainism, that preach
the importance of the moral and social values and the need for
self-restraint, in contrast to the magic sexuality of the Shambhala
tradition that we find in Tantrism. From this mysterious
kingdom, it is said, came the three Magi or wise men of the East
to worship the child Jesus. It was to some such region as this,
too, that legends may be referred concerning the enigmatic
Prester John, an unknown propagator of the Christian doctrine
who is known in the folklore of peoples living in lands stretching
from Abyssinia to China.

Urgyan

All the left-hand sects have many elements in common. Their
rites and obligations are so similar that it has not been difficult
to trace them to a common source, which has found some
acceptance among scholars. It is surmised that the leaders of the
left-hand tradition, uprooted from the Gobi kingdom, long
sought a safe refuge where they might continue their magical
pratices without interference, and finally established themselves
in a place, still not precisely identified, but thought to be
somewhere in the remote fastness of the Swat valley in north-
east Afghanistan.

In some accounts the new settlement continued to be referred to as Shambhala, after its earlier prototype. The high lamas of Tibet held the view that Shambhala was on the northern borders of India (Rao, 1977, p.132); but in the Tibetan tradition generally, this new kingdom lay outside India altogether, and was known as Urgyan (see Hoffmann, 1961), or in Indian tradition as Uddiyana. Cakravarty speaks of it as Shambalpur of Uddiyana (1963, p.93). The occult history of these remote regions is obscure, and the traditions confused, and this offers endless scope for wildly speculative theories. But the theory of an ultra-Indian origin for Tantrism in the region of Urgyan is generally accepted, even by Indian authorities.

Because of the cardinal role played by female adepts in their rituals, Urgyan was referred to as a woman's realm *(stri-rajya)*, somewhat like the Amazon nation of Greek history. The rites and conjurations associated with the sorcerous dakinis, and with the 'power-clothed' yoginis or female yogis, are said to be derived from Urgyan. The Urgyan centre was dedicated entirely to occult teachings of the left hand. There in secret enclaves were taught practical and meditative systems of phallic sorcery, black magic, yoga, mortuary and death magic, sex magic, Tantrism, yab-yum techniques, where both sexes joined in heterosexual and homosexual rites, bestiality and other perversions. Eventually these teachings were to spread far afield and profoundly influence the religious beliefs of the adjacent countries.

The famous Chinese pilgrim and traveller Hiuen-Tsang (c. A.D. 630) wrote of heretical sects in monasteries in eastern Afghanistan who made chaplets of bone and covered themselves with ashes, and of a kingdom there ruled by women (Beal, 1906). The tradition of this strange kingdom in the heart of Asia, and the marvels produced by the wonder-workers who practised there, was still alive when Western travellers began visiting these regions from the fourteenth century on.

According to Marco Polo (d. 1324), the greatest traveller of the Middle Ages, the people of Central Asia (including Tibet) were capable of performing such incredible acts of sorcery and such marvels of diabolic art that he did not deem it fit to narrate them in his book. Similar hints of marvels and demonological practices in the mysterious kingdom of Shambhala in the heart of Asia, were also recorded in the travel diaries of Catholic missionaries, such as Stephan Casella and John Cabral in the middle of the seventeenth century.

In 1735 the Dutchman Pierre van de Putte visited Central Asia and Tibet and made a record of his journey, but curiously, just before his death he burned all his notes because they were so extraordinary, and he did not want to risk being remembered as a liar.

In the middle of the nineteenth century the French abbé and missionary, Évariste Huc (d. 1860) wrote about his journey through China and Tibet, and about the wonders of the places he visited in the course of his travels. But his works were placed on the Index of Prohibited Books by the ecclesiastical authorities, and he himself was defrocked.

In more recent times, Madame Blavatsky (d. 1891), Aleister Crowley (d. 1947), Nikolai Roerich (d. 1947), George Gurdjieff (d. 1949), and Alexandra David-Neel (d. 1967), all great travellers, and some of them founders of esoteric schools, have each made their contributions to the myth of the Eastern, Central Asian or Himalayan adept.

Nikolai Roerich, Russian archaeologist, painter, philosopher and mystic, Alexandra David-Neel, French traveller and explorer in Tibet, and Ferdinand Ossendowski, scientist and traveller, all speak of Shambhala as a name to conjure with, and of its teachings as still forming part of a continuing and living tradition. Roerich in fact set up a shrine dedicated to Shambhala in Mongolia (Ashe, 1977, p.187).

Among the more important scholars and adepts who reputedly came from Urgyan or received their education there were the following: Chang Tao-Ling (c. A.D. 220) one of the founders of modern Taoism; Shenrab (c. 300), systematizer of the Bon religion of Tibet; Bogar (c. 350), founder of the Siddha sect; Bodhidharma (d. 535), founder of the Dhyana or Meditation sect; Padma-sambhava (c. 750), one of the founders of Tibetan Tantrism; Matsyendra (c. 800), founder of the Natha sect.

China
It is not clear when the stream of occult knowledge first reached China. Masters of Chinese alchemy and sexual mysticism claim to 'honour and practice the words of Huang-Lao', a composite

title combining the names of two persons. The first belongs to
Huang Ti, the mythical Yellow Emperor of China who lived in
2600 B.C. and was said to have mastered the secrets taught by the
sage Pieng-tsu relating to alchemy and breathing, and the
mysteries of absorbing the vital energies of women during
congress.

The 'Lao' in the honoured name of Huang-Lao refers to Lao
Tzu (d. 520 B.C.) one of the world's great sages and author of the
Tao Te Ching, a slender classic full of sublime wisdom. The
philosophical school founded by Lao Tzu is called Taoism, the
doctrine of the 'Way', although it was in fact a great deal older
than Lao Tzu. Perhaps a few stray words in his masterpiece
could with some difficulty be strained to reveal a sexual
significance, but otherwise the association of his name with
sexual magic, breathing techniques, Chinese sorcery and internal
alchemy, is hard to explain.

Over the centuries Taoism has drawn into its orbit all the
floating traditions of Chinese mysticism and the occult: the
doctrine of the male *(yang)* and female *(yin)* principles; the
practice of divination especially with the aid of the Chinese
classic, the *I-Ching;* the art of acupuncture; astrology and
magical almanacs; herbal lore; the making of elixirs and pills
for rejuvenation, longevity and immortality; a predilection for
forming secret societies; a special kind of concentration called
tso-wang, 'sitting with the mind blank'; control of breath *(ch'i)*
and semen *(ching);* internal alchemy.

Almost nothing of all this can be traced back to the life and
work of Lao Tzu himself, least of all the emphasis on sexual
magic. This latter innovation was first brought in by Chang Tao-
Ling (c. A.D. 220) who, refusing the enticements of the Han
court, journeyed westward across the high mountains and
studied for several years in a secret school. He returned to found
monasteries and nunneries based on an esoteric interpretation
of the teachings of Lao Tzu.

He made sexual magic a permanent feature of Taoism. The
following matters were treated by him: internal alchemy through
an understanding of esoteric physiology; heliotherapy and
moonlore – men had to expose their bodies to the morning
sunlight to invigorate the semen and *yang* essence, women had
to expose their bodies to the moon, which was supposed to

regulate the menstrual cycle (Cakravarty, 1963, p.87); the science of gaining entry into the 'jade gate' *(yiu men)* or vulva; respiratory techniques, including *ho-chi*, a 'union of breaths' during sexual intercourse; methods of coitus reservatus *(huan ching)*, or the retention of semen during intercourse.

He advocated regular sessions of group sexuality, a promiscuous hierogamy involving successive intromissions in varying postures with different women without regard to family or social status. The men were to retain their semen till they had had a number of women, the more the better, because each female orgasm *(khuai)* released a charge of energy which the partner could absorb.

Chang Tao-Ling was the real founder of modern Taoism, which became in effect a notorious new cult of sexualized Tao, with headquarters in the Lung Hu mountains in the province of Kiang Si, and his descendants ruled there till 1930, when the Red Army dispersed the retinue and unceremoniously smashed all the jars in which the Taoists claimed to have imprisoned the winds. The Chinese character for his surname, 'Chang', was used as a magical charm in China for over seventeen centuries.

Japan

The history of Tantrism in Japan is probably conterminous with its development in China. Certain tantrik concepts were embodied in the teachings found in Zen, whose historical patriarch was Bodhidharma (d. A.D. 535), a Mahayana Buddhist philosopher. Originally from the eastern Iranian plateau, he had studied in Urgyan and taught at a university in south India. From there he went to China at the invitation of the Chinese emperor.

He was believed to have been the first to set down the principles of the Dhyana (Meditation) school of Buddhism, which had a strange beginning. The story goes that one of Buddha's most famous sermons consisted in his holding up a golden-coloured flower, saying nothing. After a while one of his disciples broke into a smile, for the secret light-bearing message had dawned upon him. This 'smile of enlightenment' was passed down through twenty-eight successive patriarchs, the last being Bodhidharma who laid down its basic principles, which came to be known in Pali, the language spoken by Buddha, as Jhana.

Related to the Pali word *jhana* is the Sanskrit word *dhyana*,

from which in turn come the Chinese *ch'an* and the Japanese *zen*.
According to Theosophical lore, however, the remote ancestral
text of the Dhyana sect was actually the *Book of Dzyan*, described
as a mystical formulary, archaic, dark and confusing, and one
that eludes even the deepest study. Any such work, if it exists at
all, is quite unknown to scholars, but is said to refer back to the
two ancient sources of occult knowledge in the world, Agharti
and Shambhala. Alluding to this mysterious scripture, Madame
Blavatsky writes, 'It is a book that cannot be found; if found it
cannot be read; if read it cannot be understood'. The teachings
of the Dhyana or Zen sect are said to represent only a small and
garbled fragment of the whole doctrine.

Historically, the relation between Zen and Tantrism can be
established on a number of points. The ninth century Shingon
school of Japan is associated both with Zen and with tantrik
philosophy. Shingon, one of the most important religious sects
in Japan, is an offshoot of Vajrayana, or tantrik Buddhism, and
has an extensive tantrik iconography. Scholars have also pointed
out the closeness of Zen to *mahamudra*, one of the symbolic
procedures for mystic accomplishment (Rao, 1977, p.39).

The Shingon school makes use of mystic syllables (mantras)
in its invocations, and employs symbolic hand gestures (mudras)
and various forms of mental concentration (dhyana) derived
from tantrik yoga. Initiation of a pupil includes the ceremony of
sprinkling with water (abhisheka). Among other features that
suggest tantrik affinities in Zen we find: the idea that basic
spiritual lessons are to be learned outside the orthodox scriptures; that one need not concern oneself with right and wrong;
that intuition, spontaneity and naturalness (sahajiya) are more
important than rationality, conformity and ritualism; that the
normal human appetites, like eating and sex, are not to be
denied their proper expression; that the male-female (Shiva-
Shakti, yang-yin, yab-yum) duality, must be recognized and
reconciled in a mystical union; that for a certain higher type of
illumination, a higher kind of madness should be cultivated, and
reason annulled. Finally, as in Tantrism, the absolute authority
of the Zen guru, called the *roshi*, is unquestioned, and he is free
to abuse, kick and punch his disciples. One famous Zen master,
Ummon (d. 949) had his leg broken by his roshi during his
apprenticeship.

Tibet

The early shamanistic beliefs and demonological practices that once widely prevailed from western Asia to Siberia and Mongolia, have to some extent survived in Bon, the aboriginal, pre-Buddhist faith of Tibet. This religion was systematized and given a priesthood and a doctrine by Shenrab (c. A.D. 300), who came from the region between the Oxus and Tarim rivers, a region which shared in the Urgyan magical heritage. The followers of Bon later came to be known as the Black Hats, from the colour of the conical headgear worn during their rites.

There are nine traditional 'ways' open to a practitioner of the Bon religion, each dealing with different matters, such as oracles, imprecations, exorcism, vampirism, expersonation (dispossessing the soul from a living body and taking the body over), the propitiation of demons, and death rites. The fourth 'way', called *dur-shen* deals with the three hundred and sixty kinds of dying; with the intermediate *(bardo)* state between incarnations; with the four methods of arranging burial places; with the eighty-one methods of subduing evil spirits. There is also a secret tenth 'way', called *ma-khu-ba*, which remains unwritten, known only to a few high adepts, and 'nothing can be said about it'.

Hosts of demons are named in the Tibetan scriptures and depicted in their iconography, but detailed information about their attributes and powers is not easily available. An idea of their nature and terrifying characteristics is conveyed by Nebesky-Wojkowitz in his monumental book on the oracles and demons of Tibet. John Blofeld remarks that it is always thought unwise to write about demons at all, and adds the curious comment that Tibetans were not surprised when the author came to an untimely end soon after completing his work (1970, p.73).

In the middle of the seventh century the Tibetan royal family and the nobility were converted to Buddhism. At the end of the following century, the reigning king of Tibet, Khri-son-de-Tsan (d. A.D. 797), in order to counter the strong Chinese influence in his country, decided to invite a Buddhist theologian from India, hoping that his teaching might bring benefit to his people. Knowing about the nature of certain tantrik practices among Indian Buddhists he had first to assure the nobility and priesthood that the person invited 'would not preach obscene doctrines' (Sierksma, 1966, p.78).

The man invited was the redoubtable Padma-sambhava (c. A.D. 750), a prince of Urgyan who had visited India and taught at the Buddhist college at Nalanda. In Tibet he founded the Red Hat sect and became known as the Precious Teacher, in some circles receiving more homage than Buddha himself. But his teachings turned out to be essentially tantrik, and were said to involve demonolatrous rites and black magic, meditation in cemeteries, the taking of intoxicants and drugs, and the eating of flesh, including human flesh. But the most significant innovation was his introduction of sex ritualism in all its forms. He himself was reputed to have received his initiation from a dakini as he lay within her yoni. In Tibetan art he is depicted holding in his right hand a trident with a severed human head transfixed on it, and in his left hand a skull brimful of blood (Rao, 1977, p.17). Several Bon rites also became linked with his name.

These imported ideas were by no means well received by all Tibetans, and in that country 'tantrik' has never ceased to be identified with the abnormal and foreign. Padma-sambhava's doctrines proved to be so obnoxious that the king's chief wife, Tse-spon-bza, called a meeting of ministers to make known her distaste for this new so-called religion, whose followers use a human skull for a begging-bowl, intestines for a girdle, human skin for a mat, a human bone for a trumpet, and sprinkle blood over the altar. 'This', she concluded. 'is no religion, but the evil India has taught Tibet' (Bharati, 1965, p.172).

Yet despite attempts at reform, and the influence of orthodox sects, the attractions exerted by Bon and Tantrism have never lost their hold on the populace. The lives of the great Tibetan saints like Tilopa, Naropa and Marpa show how powerful was the dominance of these more primitive beliefs. Marpa (d. 1096) the founder of the White Hats, was a tantrik master, who openly claimed that 'lust formed part of the mystic ecstasy' (Sierksma, 1966, p.97).

Even the more orthodox lamas fell under their magic spell. The sixth Dalai Lama (d. 1706) was sympathetic to the Red Hats, and himself lived a dissolute life, given over to drunken orgies with a bevy of female companions. He did his best to revive the teachings of Padma-sambhava and the rites of sexualized Vajrayana, so much so that his cardinals reprimanded him for setting up obscene images in the holy places, for visiting brothels, for practicing sexual rites, and for desecrating the image of Buddha by shooting and stabbing at it (see Hoffmann, 1961).

To a greater or lesser degree all Tibetan sects show the influence of both Bon and Tantra. Some indeed owe little allegiance to orthodox Buddhism. The Zok-chen-pa sect, for example, is described as unmitigatedly terror-based and morbid, one of whose lamas, Padma-rig-dzin (c. 1660) made a number of bizarre elaborations on the *chod* and other graveyard ceremonies. The sorcerous Dug-pa sect of Western Tibet, with their scattered communities from Ladakh to Bhutan, is also of Bon affiliation and has acquired a notorious reputation. They are said to kidnap women and use them for sex magic (see Sharpe, 1936). Tibetan nuns of the Ka'a sect have subtle union with virile young males and employ the energy so derived for magical purposes (Garrison, 1972, p.61).

The many supernormal powers ascribed to Tibetan adepts are acquired by training in breathing techniques, by deep meditation and magical procedures, of Bon and tantrik origin. Their alleged ability to control the weather and cause rain and hail is part of Tibetan proverbial lore. In the *ro-langs* ceremony they are said to raise corpses. They practice the *chod* death rite, and immurement in caves. By mastering the *lung-gom* technique they can move along the surface of the ground with extraordinary speed in a series of long bounding steps. Through developing *tum-mo* they can control their body heat and live on snowy mountains without clothes, like the almost legendary lama Milarepa (c. 1122). By intense concentration, visualization and mental effort they can create a *tulpa* or externalized thought-form, which can on occasion assume a material appearance and carry out the wishes of its creator. Such an ideoplastic entity may be created in the shape of an alluring woman with whom the lama can have sexual congress.

India

There is some slender evidence of yogic practice in the civilization that flourished about 2000 B.C. at Harappa and

Mohenjodaro in the Indus valley. Among the clay tablets and seals of that culture we find representations of a priest gazing at the tip of his nose; of ritual gestures (mudras) and yogic postures (asanas); of a seated figure with phallus erect. Phallic worship, however, is a common feature of primitive religions, and there is no clear indication that the principles underlying later Tantrism as we know it had any part to play in these early practices. Certain elements of yogic physical culture are undoubtedly old in India, but the main features of Tantrism, especially its sexual theories and practices, are an alien importation.

Some early features of Tantrism are referred to as the 'Chinese way' *(china-chara)*, and historically many aspects of Tantrism have Chinese affinities. More specifically, the China referred to in these contexts is called Maha-china, or 'Greater China', which refers not only to China proper, but to Tibet and further west. It has been suggested that the similarities of many features of Tantrism, Taoism and other sex-oriented cults, could be accounted for by the hypothesis of their common origin in the kingdom of Urgyan.

There are several references in Sanskrit and the Indian vernaculars to the Chinese way, but few are devoted to this at any length. A text known as *Maha-china Tantra*, allegedly recorded some details of the Chinese way, but this text is no longer extant. Another text called the *Shakti-sangama Tantra*, which has a chapter on the 'method of Maha-china', may possibly contain fragments of the lost material (see Bhattacharya, 1932).

Among the scholars and adepts whose lives were associated with Urgyan and India is the semi-legendary Chinese adept and sex alchemist Bogar (c. A.D. 350), who was the founder of the Siddha and Rasavada sects of India, but of whom little is otherwise known. He is said to have been a native of China, and learned the secrets of sex alchemy from the Five Girls, the dakini-guardians of the black art pertaining to occult sexuality. He came to Urgyan for further study and to teach, and then went on to visit Persia, Arabia, Bengal and Assam (Kamarupa), finally settling in south India, teaching magic, alchemy and medicine. He made a contribution to the 'Chinese way' of Indian Tantrism.

Another major figure was Matsyendra (c. A.D. 800), known to Tibet as Lawa-pa, a native of Tag-Zigs (Tajikistan), who studied in the kingdom of Uddiyana (Urgyan), and later introduced the doctrines of the Natha sect to India. The story goes that during his sojourn in Urgyan he was so enchanted with life in the company of the free-loving women there, that he refused to leave, and was only persuaded to do so through the determined efforts of his pupil, a renowned Natha named Gorakhnath. It is thought that some of the Natha doctrines are embodied in a thirteenth-century work entitled *Kubjika Tantra*.

Sects

There are literally dozens of tantrik sects in India. Hindus and Buddhists, and to a lesser extent the Jains, each have their own forms of tantrik practice, developed according to their religious proclivities, and these again have further sectarian subdivisions.

But in spite of their differences, the *vama-charins* or followers of the left-hand path, according to D. R. Shastri, an Indian authority, 'all walk along the same track' (Desai, 1975, p.122). All these sects are antinomian; adopt an unorthodox attitude to religious and social laws; are full of occult mysteries; and advocate the dangerous 'direct path', using spells and psycho-sexual practices as a short cut to occult knowledge and magical power (siddhis).

The tantrik sects of Buddhism were among the earliest of their kind in India, the two most important being the Kalachakra and Vajrayana sects, whose texts are among the first written Tantras.

The name *Kalachakra* is made up of two words: *kala*, meaning, variously, 'black', 'time', 'death', or 'fate'; and *chakra*, meaning 'wheel'. The doctrine most probably originated in Urgyan (see Bharati, 1965, p.222) and is strongly antinomian, but to lend it authority it was ascribed to a sermon given by Buddha in south India towards the end of his life. This sermon was heard by the king of Shambhala (Urgyan) who on returning to his native country recorded and preserved the text.

The term *Vajrayana* is made up of the words *vajra*, which means 'diamond', or 'thunderbolt', and has a sublime connotation in Buddhism generally, but in Tantrism also refers to the phallus; and *yana*, meaning 'way' or 'method'. Vajrayana teaches a highly sexualized form of tantrik Buddhism.

The Hindu tantrik or tantrik-inspired sects have been even

more prolific and widespread. Although at one level many of these sects remain within the orthodox lines of Hinduism, the more extreme left-hand sects have been notorious for their unorthodox and antinomian character. Many acquired an evil reputation for sorcery, necrophilia, human sacrifice, murder, cannibalism, scatophagy (filth-eating), the use of intoxicants and drugs, promiscuous and perverse sexuality, and various forms of left-hand occultism.

In Sanskrit dramas these latter sects, often named in a general and not sectarian context, were portrayed in situations intended to arouse the emotions *(bhava)* of terror, disgust, anger and horror. Listed below are a few of the more important of these sects. It is to be noted that some are no longer known by the names once used for them, but their practices are still carried on.

The *Shaivites* are named after the god Shiva, and the *Shaktas* after his consort Shakti. The *Kaulas*, a broad designation, include those who owe their affiliation to the sectarian family *(kula)* of the goddess Kali. The *Sauras* are named after the sun god Surya, but devotion is actually paid to Shani (Saturn), the son of Surya and Chhaya (Shadow). Shani, known as 'the evil-eyed one', is usually shown robed in black and riding on a vulture. The *Ganapatyas* are devotees of Ganapati or Ganesh, the Hindu elephant-headed deity. According to legend the god Shiva and his spouse seeing a pair of elephants mating, decided to enjoy each other 'in the elephant mode'; they took on elephant shape and had intercourse, as a result of which their son Ganapati was born with an elephant head.

The *Lakulishas* worship Shiva as 'Lord of the Club', that is, the phallus. The *Pashupatas* worship him as 'Lord of the Beasts'. The cult of the cannibalistic *Aghoris* was founded by Kanipa; the *Siddhas* by Bogar; the *Nathas* by Matsyendranath; the *Kanphatas* or 'ear-torn' ones, by Goraknath. The ear-cartilage of the members of the last-named sect was perforated on initiation to permit the insertion of enormous earrings. The *Shavavadins* or cadaverists, are preoccupied with corpses and graveyards. Associated with them are the *Kalamukhas* or 'black-faced ones'; the *Kapalikas* or skullists, who operate with the aid of a human skull; and the *Shepalas*, from *shepa*, 'phallus', whose members wear an iron ring attached to the sexual organ. The Shepalas claim the power to control scorpions, snakes, jackals and other creatures, whose flesh they eat. Some snake-charmers and conjurers belong to this sect.

Bengal

The word 'Tantra' in a context suggesting a doctrinal theory was unknown in India in the fifth century A.D. But by the eighth century the names of sixty-four Tantras are mentioned.

The spread of Tantrism in the Indian subcontinent has not yet been clearly traced, but is known to have been very rapid. From present evidence it appears to have spread from Urgyan to the border districts of north-west India, via Kashmir along the Himalayan foothills, southwards to the Deccan, and eastwards to Bengal and Assam. Desai says that Tantrism 'spread like a wild fire in all the regions of India' (1975, p.126).

But it was in the east that it found its most hospitable milieu. The peoples of these eastern territories were described by the orthodox Hindu lawgivers as impure and unclean because of the vile nature of their customs, and the lands where they lived were treated as beyond the pale for the righteous.

Because Tantrism in India was so closely linked with Bengal, certain scholars hold that the Tantras are a product of Bengal (Dutt, 1979, p.i.). Their dynastic lines of kings, the Palas (A.D. 760-1142) and Senas (1095-1119) founded the famous tantrik universities of Udantapura, Vikramashila, Somapura and Jagadalla. In Orissa, Assam and south India too, the royal courts had tantrik ministers and astrologer-advisers.

Tantrik practices flourished 'on a grand scale' (Douglas, 1971, p.12) throughout Eastern India until the beginning of the thirteenth century, when the Muslim invaders began their incursions into the region and discovered what was being taught at these colleges. Closer acquaintance confirmed their view that these centres were hotbeds of secret vice and moral corruption, and their teachings unworthy of perpetuation or remembrance. They slew the monks, burned the libraries, destroyed thousands of licentious books and works of erotic art, and razed the monasteries to the ground. So effectively was this done that even the site of some of these once famous seats of learning remains untraceable today.

Much of what is known of tantrik doctrine has been gleaned

from translations of tantrik writings made in Nepal, Tibet,
China and other places outside India, though of course a great
deal continued to be secretly transmitted, particularly in Bengal,
whose reputation as a stronghold of Tantrism continued
unabated through the succeeding centuries.

In 1690 the Englishman Job Charnock, stationed in Bengal,
saved a young Indian widow from being burned on the funeral
pyre of her husband, and later married her. He settled near the
temple *ghat* of the goddess Kali, the terror-aspect of Shakti.
Here, on Charnock's recommendation, the factories of the East
India Company were set up, to grow in time into the city of
Calcutta, anglicized from Kali-ghat, which was eventually to
become the capital of India, and, after London, the second city
of the British empire.

In the Western world Calcutta was often associated with
idolatry at its most corrupt and abhorrent, and its ill-repute was
reflected in the often sensational reports provided by European
writers. Gabriel Jogand-Pages (d. 1907), French writer, also
known by his pen-name of Leo Taxil, was the editor and part
author, under yet another pen-name, Dr Bataille, of a
voluminous and highly popular work entitled *The Devil in the
Nineteenth Century* (1894), a fanciful report on the headquarters
of Satanism in various parts of the world.

In his lurid account the haunts of Eastern diabolism are
described as places of putrefaction and vice. The centres of
worship, he writes, were dedicated without concealment to the
ghastly phantasms of mankind's worst nightmares, to
debauchery, filth, animality and prostitution. Here, in temples
infested with rodents and cockroaches and watched over by the
circling vultures, the 'winged lingam' was worshipped by
emaciated sadhus in attitudes of unbelievable contortion, their
flesh covered in ulcers and stinking as if they were afflicted with
gangrene.

This 'charnel-house asceticism' was the result of their self-
imposed surrender to the denizens of the nether regions who
were the objects of their devotions, and the cruel rites associated
with their worship.

Bataille and other Western writers reserved their most
virulent diatribes for Calcutta, which was dubbed 'the city of
living death and universal corruption'. A humid, hellish, fever-

ridden place, held in thrall by one of the most monstrous forms of deity ever conceived by man, and suffering in consequence from cataclysm, plague, fanaticism and civil strife. It was, in their eyes, a carrion place where men if not vigilant would merge with the putresence of the stinking soil.

To many outsiders, this unhappy caricature remains an accurate account of this once great and beautiful metropolis.

6.

TANTRA IN THE WEST

In the history of Western occult societies, a link real or contrived can often be found with some esoteric system of the East. These include the Hermetics, Gnostics, Alchemists, Kabalists, Templars, Freemasons, Martinists, Rosicrucians and other illuminati. Directly or indirectly the religions and cults of Asia have exerted a far-reaching influence not only on the secret societies of the west, but on its art and politics as well.

The complex ramifications of the subject make a detailed examination impossible here, and we shall confine ourselves mainly to a brief list, a mere catalogue, of some of the better-known personalities in the Occident to whose theories and practices an Oriental provenance, often with tantrik overtones, may be ascribed.

Traditionally, a number of European adepts who taught occult truths were said to have travelled to and received some kind of illumination in 'the East'. Foremost among them were: the semi-legendary Christian Rosenkreutz (d. 1484) who visited the fabled and unidentified city of Damcar, probably somewhere in the Middle East, and returned to Germany to set up the Rosicrucian fraternity; the celebrated Swiss-German alchemist and occultist Theophrastus Paracelsus (d. 1541), who allegedly visited the Cham of Tartary; the enigmatic Comte de Saint-Germain (d. 1784?) who was said to have travelled to India and learnt Sanskrit; Count Alessandro di Cagliostro (d. 1795), founder of an influential masonic order, who spent many years in the orient.

The first serious studies of Eastern wisdom began with the eighteenth century, when the great British, French and German orientalists embarked on their pioneering work of translation and commentary, often at second hand.

The French scholar Antoine Leonard de Chézy (d. 1832) mastered Sanskrit without a teacher and without ever going to India, and became the first Professor of Sanskrit at the Collège de France. The German-born British scholar Friedrich Max-Müller (d. 1900) published a vast number of books of Indian interest, though he himself never set foot in India either. This is reminiscent of the scholarship of Sir James Frazer (d. 1941) who wrote massive and authoritative works on the cultures of the primitive tribes of the world, and when asked whether he had ever seen any of the peoples about whom he had written so learnedly replied, 'God forbid!'.

But there were scores of others who studied the Indian, Tibetan, Chinese and Japanese classics at first hand, and in the countries concerned. A lesser number investigated the more arcane and, at the time, more tabooed aspects of Eastern religions, but their writings were largely ignored by more conservative scholars. Among the latter was Edward Sellon (who committed suicide in 1866), who lived in India for ten years and wrote one of the earliest detailed expositions of Tantrism.

Another was Sir John Woodroffe, a judge of the Calcutta High Court and a Roman Catholic, who during the first two decades of the present century translated texts and wrote extensive commentaries on Shaktism, in his own name as well as under the pseudonym, Arthur Avalon. He found resemblances between Roman Catholic and Hindu religious rites (1972, p.xii).

Not all those who came to India to learn were impressed by what they found. Quite a few dismissed the plethora of gods and godlings and had little time for popular Hinduism in practice. Laurence Oliphant (below) found the Hindu religions and their idols offensive. Aleister Crowley disliked India and 'its torment of damned souls', as he put it with characteristic bluntness, and referred to the Ganges as 'a river of hell'. Buddhism, he said, 'got on my nerves'. Aldous Huxley (d. 1963) wrote, 'India is depressing as no other country in the world. One breathes in it not air, but dust and hopelessness.'

What really stimulated the interest of many students of the Orient, besides its religion and philosophy, were the ventures made in personal, psychic and spiritual development, and the whole field of Eastern mysticism, particularly in relation to sexuality. This interest was rife both in Europe and America, and those who went in for such studies were often tempted to evolve their own system as a result.

In America one of the earliest pioneers of a sex doctrine with a tantrik flavour was Paschal Beverly Randolph (d. 1875), an occultist of part Negro origin. He travelled widely, visited many places in the East, and produced a book on sex magic that was to have a great influence via his European disciples, on the famous occult order known as the OTO, to be considered later. Randolph used psychedelic drugs in his sex-magic rituals.

Another well-known sex mystic was the English-born American Thomas Lake Harris (d. 1906) who wrote a book on the evolution of man in four ages, starting with the past golden age, and ending with the present iron age, when the sinister creeds of Chaldea, Persia, China and India will be spread abroad. But his own theories and practices, according to one writer, 'bear some resemblance to tantrik yoga' (Colquhoun, 1975, p.292) and involve breathing exercises combined with sexual intercourse without ejaculation.

Among Harris's pupils was the English statesman, traveller, occultist, and one-time special correspondent of *The Times*, Laurence Oliphant (d. 1888), who visited India and several other places in the east. He later broke away from Harris, and he and his beautiful wife ended their career in Palestine, where he developed a method of internal respiration related to yogic breath-control, called *sympneumata*, to be practised by both partners during sexual intercourse. They regarded themselves as 'sex missionaries', and used to demonstrate their sysem in action to the local Arabs and Jews (Strachey, 1928).

In France a growing interest in Oriental occultism can be discerned from about a century after the establishment of the French East India Company in 1664, when the work of the French indologists was beginning to become more popularly known. Here one of the early pioneers was Antoine Fabre d'Olivet (d. 1825) who was fascinated with the East, and wrote a highly imaginative occult history of the world going back some 12,000 years, wherein he described the flooding of Atlantis and its mainly black and red populations, and the emergence of a superior white race somewhere around the north pole led by a personage called Ram.

Ram, which is the name of a Hindu god-hero, and his counterpart Ram-Manu (Manu, the name of the progenitor of mankind, and also of a Hindu lawgiver) continued to appear in the works of a number of French occultists, notably Joseph Alexandre Saint-Yves d'Alveydre (d. 1909) who claimed to have been initiated into the mysteries of Hinduism by a brahmin pundit and to be in telepathic communication with the then Dalai Lama. In his writings he mentions Agharti, the underground city which in occult tradition is believed to be a focus of superior wisdom.

The practical application of occult knowledge, especially of the more blatantly left-hand variety, was demonstrated in the activities of a succession of nineteenth century black magicians, defrocked priests among them, such as: the sorcerer and mage Pierre-Michel Eugène Vintras (d. 1875); the French abbé, Joseph-Antoine Boullan (d. 1893); and the Belgian abbé, Louis van Haecke (d. 1912). They performed the Black Mass, blasphemed God and preached and practised salvation through sexuality, with particular emphasis on adultery, incest, sodomy, masturbation and bestiality. Astral entities were allegedly invoked during their rites for the purpose of spectral intercourse with them, as well as with the *humanimaux*, elemental creatures half animal and half human, that were brought into being through mating with animals.

The Kabalist Marie Victor Stanislas de Guaita (d. 1897) began prying into the affairs of the Satanist Boullan and instigated a campaign against him, and, in tantrik fashion, a regular 'battle of the sorcerers' ensued, with each party trying to exterminate the other by means of black magic. Boullan, it would appear, got the worst of the encounter, for he collapsed and died suddenly in an agonizing fit. The French novelist Joris Karl Huysmans (d. 1907), who personally knew many of the protagonists of the black magical organisations of his day, embodied a great deal of factual information about them in his novels, and he too, it was said, ended his days in horrible suffering as a result.

The Western occult trail if followed back to its sources, does not always lead one to India, for strong Chinese, Tibetan and Central Asian influences form an integral part of the tradition.

Perhaps the best known exponent of this latter branch was

the Russian-Buriat mystic, George Gurdjieff (d. 1949), who travelled widely in Mongolia and Tibet, and studied in various monasteries there. At one of these centres he studied the teachings of Mehmet Karagöz (d. 1805), an almost legendary figure and probably the last of the great mages of Tartary. Gurdjieff was also influenced by the ideas of Shamzaran Badmaev (d. 1919) a Buriat-Mongol physician who had mastered Chinese, Mongolian and Tibetan medicine, specialized in female physical and mental disorders, and served as medical adviser to the Tsarist court before the rise of Gregory Rasputin.

After his travels Gurdjieff settled near Paris, where he gained a remarkable ascendency over a large number of disciples, including many intellectuals, although not all who met him were impressed. Some declared that like other Eastern gurus he demanded and received abject docility, and reduced his pupils to robot-like obedience by intimidation, insult, threat, vile abuse and even physical violence.

His sexual behaviour was said to have been wild and un-controlled, and several of his pupils bore him children. It has been suggested that his erotic activities stemmed from the secret sexual techniques, perhaps a form of Tantrism, he had learned in the East. The chief character in Gurdjieff's *magnum opus* is Beelzebub, and he himself has been variously described by his detractors as a devil-possessed wizard, a protégé of Satan, and the incarnation of Lucifer.

An organization that seems to have brought together all the main clues of the Eastern esoteric, though not distinctively tantrik, tradition, and whose founding is a landmark in the history of the occult, is the Theosophical Society, whose chief architect was Madame Helena Petrovna Blavatsky (d. 1891). A great traveller, she claimed to have entered Tibet, a country closed to foreigners, and been initiated in a monastery there in 1867.

She wrote, sometimes under the influence of hashish, several books filled with esoteric lore, which owed a great deal to Hindu and Buddhist systems of thought, and brought to public awareness in the West such concepts as karma, prana, kundalini, yoga and reincarnation. She popularized the theory of root races, the Great White Brotherhood, adepts, chiefs, mahatmas, and other teachers of secret wisdom who dwell in non-corporeal form in the Gobi desert and the Himalayan fastnesses.

On the death of Madame Blavatsky the mantle of theosophical leadership fell on the shoulders of Mrs Annie Besant (d. 1933), who on joining the society changed from being an uncompromising atheist into accepting unequivocally the pantheon of the Hindus. Like Blavatsky she was virulent in her attacks on Christianity which, she said, 'the Chiefs regard as particularly pernicious'.

The Society came in for rough handling both in India and the West. The founder, it was said, produced faked letters from the Mahatmas to endorse her activities. Scandals were also associated with some of its leaders and their homosexual tendencies, notably Charles Webster Leadbeater (d. 1934), who in a notorious case was charged with unnatural acts with boys.

It was alleged by some that in the higher Theosophical circles Satan and Lucifer had become names of power. The French esotericist René Guénon (d. 1951) believed that the Theosophical Society might be the tool of more insidious and sinister forces. William Quan Judge, secretary of the Society's American section, thought Mrs Besant was under the influence of the dark powers. Rudolf Steiner (d. 1925), who had himself been secretary general of the German section of the organization, felt that Theosophy was a subversive movement that sprang from the great subterranean world of evil and heralded the coming of the Satanic age (Pauwels and Bergier, 1963, p.152).

Others suggested that the Satanic age was ushered in when the sexual nature of the unconscious was brought to light by Sigmund Freud and his followers. One of Freud's disciples was Wilhelm Reich (d. 1957), who was interested in Buddhism and much impressed by the writings of Rudolf Steiner. Reich claimed he had discovered the physical basis of the libido in what he called orgone energy which, he maintained, was a visible and measurable substance. Nik Douglas thinks that during his researches into orgone energy Reich had 'undoubtedly stumbled upon the all-powerful kundalini-shakti, which has its roots in the sexual centres' (1971, p.53).

Another society, with more openly tantrik affiliations than those so far mentioned, was started by a wealthy Viennese freemason, Karl Kellner (d. 1905) who, inspired by the work of P. B. Randolph (above), travelled extensively in the east and acquired certain secrets of the left-hand path from an adept in Arabia and two tantriks in India. He returned to Europe to found in 1902 the Ordo Templi Orientis (OTO), the Order of the Temple of the Orient, based principally on sex magic. The 'temple' referred to was not that of King Solomon, central to the rites of the freemasons, but 'probably commemorated the Hindu fane' where Kellner studied the elements of tantrik sex magic (Colquhoun, 1975, p.29).

Early members of the OTO included Rudolf Steiner (d. 1925), who later founded Anthroposophy; Gérard Encausse (d. 1916), a French occultist who made a study of Hindu scriptures and wrote voluminously under the pen-name of 'Papus'; Gerald Brousseau Gardner (d. 1964) who spent many years in the East, and became the founder of English neo-witchcraft, with emphasis on nudity, flagellation and sex.

Aleister Crowley

The most notable member of the OTO group was Aleister Crowley (d. 1947), who was also a member of another famous occult organization, the Hermetic Order of the Golden Dawn. He is a formidable figure in the history of European occultism, with a reputation to match that of Michael Scot, Cornelius Agrippa, Dr Johann Faust and other fabled magicians of the past.

Crowley's travels took him to North Africa, Egypt, India, Tibet, Nepal, Burma, Indochina and China. While in Calcutta he sacrificed a goat to the goddess Kali. He evolved his own brand of ritual, often requiring the use of scatological substances. He took drugs throughout his life, opium, ether, cocaine, hashish, morphine, and firmly believed in the possibility of some 'pharmaceutical' method of inducing samadhi and mystical experience. His magical operations were aided by a succession of chief priestesses on whom he bestowed the satanic title (Rev. 17.4) of Scarlet Woman. But he had a low opinion of women in general and thought they should be made public property.

Sex was absolutely basic to Crowley's ceremonial magic, and his approach was tantrik. He advocated: fornication before and outside the marriage; intercourse with virgins; anal and oral intercourse; intercourse during the menses of the female;

autosexuality, homosexuality; beastiality. He said he never picked his women for their beauty; he preferred old and ugly women because it demonstrated that he performed his sex magic in a purely 'metaphysical' way.

Several occultists of lesser standing were associated with Crowley. Among them was the Scotsman Allan Bennett (d. 1924), Roman Catholic, Theosophist, member of the Golden Dawn. In Ceylon Bennett studied Vedanta but discarded it as nebulous, turned to Buddhism and became a Buddhist monk, although he retained a firm belief in the terrifying power of Shiva. He was supposed to have acquired the ability to levitate. He regularly took drugs, opium, morphine, cocaine, chloroform, and died in a London garret.

One of Crowley's most gifted protégés was Victor Neuburg (d. 1940), Jewish-born British occultist, who became first a pupil and then a partner of Crowley's in his homosexual magic. His use of mandalas and mantras, especially the mystical syllable Om, and of sexual rites calling for the magical use of semen, are again purely tantrik in origin. Later in life, after he had abandoned magic, Neuburg assumed the role of literary god-father to Dylan Thomas, whose talent he discovered and whose poems he helped to launch.

Among other associates of the Crowley group were Charles Stansfeld Jones, Wilfred T. Smith, and John W. Parsons. Parsons himself was also a friend of Lafayette Ron Hubbard, to whom he allegedly disclosed the psycho-sexual magical techniques of the highest grades of the OTO, although Hubbard was not an initiate of the order. Hubbard, too, travelled to the East, where he studied mysticism and eventually founded scientology, though this has nothing to do with the OTO.

There were several other lesser-known figures who carried on the left-hand tradition. Mrs Editha Anna Jackson (d. 1910), also known as 'Madame Horus', an American of German-Spanish origin, along with her husband Frank Dutton Jackson, started an occult institute in London, with rituals based partly on those of the Golden Dawn, teaching *congressus subtilis* and sex magic borrowed from Hindu Tantrism. They were brought to trial in 1901, but owing to the gross indecency of the evidence no record of the court proceedings was made. The nature of the acts committed during the rites was such that *The Lancet* found the details 'too revolting to relate'. The pair were sentenced to penal servitude.

Austin Osman Spare (d. 1956), occultist, member of the Golden Dawn, and brilliant graphic artist, fell under the influence of a Mrs Patterson, who claimed descent from a witch of Salem and who gave him instruction in sex magic and the methods of acquiring astral vision and 'glamour'. Although she was old and far from beautiful she reputedly had the power of taking on the semblance of seductive beauty. Spare spoke of the reality of having intercourse in the astral with incubi and succubi. His own mysticism was based on meditation and visualization while in various ritual attitudes, including the postures of sexuality and death.

The Nazis

In 1904 Crowley published a book, entitled *Liber Legis*, 'the book of the law', which he claimed had been mysteriously dictated to him, and he stated that the nation that adopted its principles would dominate the world. A German translation of the book was said to have been sent to Hitler, and Crowley later declared that Hitler often quoted from and paraphrased this work (King, 1976, p.141).

The link between the Nazis and the occult has been the subject of several works (Ravenscroft, 1972; Brennan, 1974; Angebert, 1975; Webb, 1976; King, 1976, among others). Much of the material available on this, the shadow side of modern Western civilization, still needs sorting out, but it is generally agreed that those who see in National Socialism nothing more than a fascist political movement know only a small part of the full story.

Speaking of the rising tide of the Nazi movement, D. H. Lawrence (d. 1930) wrote, 'The great leaning of the Germanic spirit now is towards the strange vortex of Tartary'. Between the two World Wars, Germany was riddled with occultism, and many of those who rose to prominence in the Nazi party were drawn to occult groups. Rudolf Hess, for example, was a disciple of Rudolf Steiner, and Alfred Rosenberg attempted to put into practice the ideas of George Gurdjieff. But the roots of the Nazi party itself go back to a number of racially-biased organizations and individuals, of which only a few can be mentioned here.

One of the earliest was the Order of the New Templars, founded in 1907 by Jörg Lanz von Liebenfels, which sponsored the idea of the superiority of the 'Ario-heroic' master race of Germany, and used the swastika as its symbol. The twenty-year-old Hitler visited von Liebenfels in Vienna in 1909 to collect copies of his anti-Jewish occult periodicals.

Another anti-Semitic group, the German Order, flourished between 1912 and 1923, inspired by the ideas of Guido von List (d. 1919), a Viennese occultist. It claimed to be a continuation of a Germanic order founded in the Middle Ages, substituted the swastika for the cross, and included perverse sex activities in its rituals.

Also engaged in anti-Semitic propaganda at this time was Dietrich Eckhart (d. 1923), poet, historian, drug addict, satanist and magician, well versed in the kind of sex magic taught by Crowley. Eckhart claimed to have initiated Hitler after having opened and enlivened his psychic centres or chakras. Shortly before his death he said, 'Follow Hitler. He will dance, but it is I who have called the tune.'

The Edelweiss Society, an offshoot of the Golden Dawn but with a Nordic direction, saw signs of the imminent appearance of a Nordic messiah and fervently awaited his advent. In 1921 Hermann Göring joined the society as an active member.

The Luminous Lodge with headquarters in Berlin, included in its membership German occultists, Japanese Buddhists, Gurdjieff students, Rosicrucians, Tibetan lamas, Indian yoga adepts, as well as members of the Golden Dawn and the OTO.

The German elements of the Luminous Lodge were subsequently detached and absorbed within the Ahnenerbe, 'ancestral heritage', a Nazi occult bureau devoted to research into the past achievements of the Indo-Germanic race. It was directed by a German expert in Sanskrit who began each meeting with yoga meditation.

The Ahnenerbe in turn became a branch of the most satanic of the Nazi appendages, the SS (Schutzstaffel), nicknamed the Black Order (Schwarze Orden), headed by Heinrich Himmler. This organization was thoroughly occult in character. It has been suggested that the mass exterminations in the concentration camps were initially of a ritual nature with the magic significance of human sacrifices (Pauwels and Bergier, 1963, p.199).

Finally, The Thule Society, named from Ultima Thule of
ancient mythology (see page 88), appears to have been started
some time in 1920. Its founder, Rudolf von Sebottendorff, a
member of the German Order (above) whose real name was
Rudolf Glauer, was influenced by the writings of Blavatsky. He
lived in Turkey for twelve years during which time he read
Oriental philosophy and practised Eastern meditation techniques.

Along with their racist and mystical ideology and the theory
of the hollow earth, the Thulists advanced certain secret power-
principles allegedly derived from the magical *Book of Dzyan*,
and communicated to them through a group of Tibetans, of
whom about three thousand were then living in Berlin. At this
time too in Germany there was a higher rate of Hindu gurus per
capita than in the US today (Wilson and Weldon, 1980, p.54).
The Thule Society promulgated a Nordic variety of yoga,
evolved by Siegfried Kummer, in which they practised bodily
postures in the shape of the ancient runic alphabet.

The swastika symbol had already been adopted by more than
one Germanophil organization, but the Thule Society used it in
its so-called inverted form, that is, with the left arm raised and
bent over, the other spokes following in the same direction,
signifying, in occult terms, the left-hand path, and this became
the official Nazi emblem.

The membership of this exclusive society comprised judges,
police chiefs, barristers, university professors, aristocrats,
industrialists, doctors, scientists. Among them was Karl
Haushofer, a student of Oriental philosophy who studied
Sanskrit and Japanese in the East. He was also interested in the
occult and was friendly with Gurdjieff. Expanding on the
geopolitical theories of Friedrich Rätzel, which related historical
development to the geographical environment, Haushofer
stated that whoever controlled the heartland of Central Asia
would achieve unassailable world supremacy. This was based on
the occult belief that Shambhala and Agharti in Inner Asia,
constituted the central mystic source of world power. It is
noteworthy that both Shambhala and Agharti were mentioned
during the Nuremberg war crimes trials of 1945-46 (Ashe, 1977,
p.168), and that several Nazi leaders subscribed to the hollow
earth theory.

It was towards Adolf Hitler that many ambitious individuals in these groups seem to have directed their efforts, for they saw in him the fulfilment of all their hopes. Hitler too saw himself as a man of destiny. On one occasion he confided to Hermann Rauschning, governor of Dantzig, 'I will tell you a secret. I am founding an order'. He also made clear his purpose in doing so, 'I am freeing men from the dirty and degrading chimera of conscience and morality'.

Many people who met Hitler at the time felt he was a man possessed and devil-led, the creature of the powers of darkness. Some suspected that he dabbled in black magic. Indeed, there were those even among his own followers who echoed the same feeling. Alfred Jodl, Nazi general, said of Hitler at the Nuremberg trials, 'He was a great man, but of the Inferno'.

Writing of the possessed Hitler, the degenerate Göring and the fanatical Goebbels, the psychologist C. G. Jung remarked, 'Any single partner of this unlucky trinity would be enough to make anyone, whose instincts are not warped, cross himself thrice'.

Together these standard bearers of the Kali yuga changed the face of the world.

Tantra and Pop
Students of the subject repeatedly affirm that Tantrism is a way of life. No declaration of allegiance need be made to it; a person may be a tantrik without knowing it.

Tantra is the outlook of the Kali yuga. Its 'vibes' are in the air, to be picked up by anyone ready to receive them. In the West they have distinctive overtones, appropriate to what has been called the New Dark Ages.

Ajit Mookerjee, a leading authority on Tantra art says, 'The frustration of the Western youth which today yearns for the mysteries of the universe has already opened a mental door by which Tantrism enters their life' (1977, p.7). This would apply more specifically to those people who by temperament are susceptible to occult influences, such as artists and musicians, especially the young and impressionable.

Here again it is not possible to deal at any length with this vast and interesting subject, but a few points of significance may be mentioned.

The landmarks of the popular post-war youth movements in the West may be traced from the beatniks in the 1950s, to the hippies in the 1960s and the punks and their variants in the 1970s. Perhaps unconsciously, perhaps intentionally, they picked up and took over many of the tokens marking an Eastern alliance. Mookerjee, quoted above, speaks of the striking similarities he finds 'between some tantrik works and objects of art, and various styles and symbols that are current in contemporary art' (1977, p.6).

The beads, bells and incense, sitar music and the tabla, the chanting of mantras and cross-legged meditation, are clearly of Oriental origin; but the debt to the East can equally be traced through the more obscure symbolizations in personal appearance, behaviour and jargon.

The punks wear safety-pins through their noses, cheeks and ears, which is reminiscent of the spikes and ear-rings of the ear-split *(kan-phata)* yogis and tantrik sadhus. The shaven pates of the skinheads, the long unkempt locks of the acidheads, the spiked hair, Afro hairstyles, Mohican haircuts and Rasta 'dreadlocks' of other groups suggest the top-knots, matted hair and tonsures of the Shaivite ascetics. The striped faces daubed with paint, the mottoes on badges and emblazoned on T-shirts are analogous to sectarian caste-marks and cultic insignia. Some of the expletives in common usage might have been lifted straight from the formulary of maledictions in the tantrik grimoires: Get knotted! Get lost! Drop dead!

Writing in 1971 Robert Bloch noted that more and more certain elements among the hippies practise sorcery and celebrate rites that 'parallel Crowley's acts of sex magic' (in Haining, 1971, p.16). The titles assumed by some popular youth groups are perhaps designed to suggest more than a predilection for the sinister image: Satan's Slaves and Hell's Angels. Likewise the aliases adopted by some prominent Punk musicians: Paul Grotesque, Sid Vicious, Johnny Rotten.

Many groups do not resent and in fact welcome being designated freaks, punks, dropouts and weirdos. Their attitude is profane in the original meaning, 'outside the *fanum* or temple', for their dedication is to everything unorthodox. Their provocative life-style, their insistence on doing their own thing, their sexual permissiveness, their opposition to the Establishment and to all intellectual 'artsy-fartsy' is genuine tantra.

From the beginning the pop groups have indulged in social and political comment. But over the years their allegiance has not been consistent, and they have moved from pacifism to passive resistance, then sometimes to active resistance and violence; and this violence has been in support both of the extreme left and the extreme right. Their emblems are as much the hammer and sickle as the swastika.

Their rebellion is further emphasized by their adoption of drugs as a way of life. There is probably no area of modern life where the use of drugs is more pervasive than in the field of the arts. With few exceptions, the protagonists of the pop scene are drug dependent. Symbolically, drugs as a way out have also been used as a means of romantic self-destruction, either through excess or deliberate suicide. This strange preoccupation with death led some hippies of the 1960s to hold their own funeral ceremonies, again reminiscent of tantrik graveyard rituals.

From being a symbol of their rebellion, drugs also betokened their conversion to a new faith, even where there was no open affiliation to Zen, Subud, Sufism, Tao, Yoga, TM or Tantra. Drugs offered a short cut to xenophrenia, to a kind of trance-like experience not provided by orthodoxy. The pop jargon for states analogous to 'samadhi' is almost as varied as that of Eastern mysticism: getting stoned, getting high, getting turned on, taking a trip, freaking out, blowing the mind, all synonyms for the condition of psychedelic nirvana experienced by the questing young, and not so young, sadhaks, sannyas, tantriks and swamis of the West.

The US high priest of the drug scene of the 1960s was Timothy Leary, who described his reaction after taking a hallucinogenic drug, as 'the deepest religious experience of my life'. In true tantrik fashion he exhorted his followers to 'turn on, tune in, and drop out'. He proclaimed that the goal of the LSD session is 'to discover and make love with God, to discover and make love with yourself, and to discover and make love with a woman' (Parrinder, 1976, p.180).

Agehananda Bharati, Austrian-born Catholic turned tantrik sadhu, believes that the hippies and freaks are also closer to true mysticism than orthodox Hindus of the Vedantic persuasion. He was greatly impressed with the personality of Allen Ginsberg,

guru of the US beat scene, student of the *Bhagavad-gita*, Buddhism,
Zen and Tantra, and compared him with Jesus Christ. Ginsberg
for his part compared the Fugs, a pop group of the 1960s to
Jesus Christ. Taking over the mantle for his own group, the
Beatles, John Lennon said, 'Kids are more influenced by us than
by Jesus'. A comment made about the Rolling Stones reflects a
similar view: 'If Jesus Christ came to town, he wouldn't sell more
tickets' (Botts, 1980, p.112).

The near deification of pop stars is a corollary of the fervent
homage they receive from their fans, once again a word derived
from *fanum*, 'temple', and signifying the enthusiastic ('god-
filled') devotion of the devotees. On occasion the concert halls
functioned as the new temples, and disabled people and epileptics
were sometimes brought backstage after a Beatles concert to be
given a touch of their healing hands (Morrison, 1981, p.547).

Protest against social restraint and against the conventional
mores is a constant theme of pop music. Equally, sexual
symbolism has frequently been read into many aspects of its
performance, some covert, some clear even to the most
unfreudian. Lawrence Lipton says that four-letter words are
taboo with the beat, though not in the sense of forbidden, but in
the Samoan sense of holy. Critics have pointed out that in some
groups lewdness and obscenity are all-pervasive. One authority
went so far as to observe that rock music is about 'f...ing and
that's all it's about' (Jasper, 1972, p.123).

In tantrik terms, the pop singer gripping his microphone
might be the Western equivalent of the *danda-pani* (phallus
holder). The grimaces, gesticulations and pelvic gyrations
vividly mime the actions of sexual intercourse. Jim Morrison (d.
1971), self-styled king of orgasmic rock, of whom one of his
biographers said that he 'was a god' (Hopkins and Sugerman,
1980), was charged in Miami in 1969 with exposing his private
parts and simulating masturbation and oral copulation (Webb,
1975, p.327).

Many of these tantra-like features were more overtly captured
in certain avant-garde films made by post-war film producers.
The following are a few titles from what could be expanded into
a lengthy inventory: *Fireworks* (1947) by Kenneth Anger, a film
of sado-masochistic homosexual encounters; *Flesh of Morning*
(1956), a masturbation fantasy by Stanley Brakhage; Jack

Smith's *Flaming Creatures* (1963), which depicts a transvestite orgy; *Sodoma* (1969) by Otto Mühl, described as 'an orgy of tortures and destructive anally-obsessed sex' (Curtis, 1971, p.154); John Lennon's *Self-Portrait* shows his penis in partial and full erection for fifteen minutes; whilst in *Performance* (1970), Mick Jagger, his girl friend and another man have a nude threesome on a large bed.

Blow Job (1964), named from the slang term for oral-genital stimulation, is a thirty-minute fellatio episode made by Andy Warhol, US painter, film-producer and one of the pillars of the pop generation. His *Fuck (Blue Movie)* (1969) focuses on a coital act in its entirety. The same artist's play *Pork* (1971) featured simulated acts of masturbation, fornication, homosexuality and defecation (Webb, 1975, p.341). It is an axiom of Tantrism, that what is natural cannot be wrong.

That the drawing appeal of such shows has attracted the attention of more established producers is evident from *Last Tango in Paris* (1972), produced by Bernado Bertolucci, where some of these motifs were given a kind of artistic status and drew favourable comment from reputable critics. This film includes a scene in which the man uses butter to facilitate an act of sodomy on the woman, and another in which he orders her to put her finger up his anus (Webb, 1975, p.295).

Speaking of the underground film producers, Renan says, 'Many film-makers believe in the supernatural, several are practicing occultists' (1968, p.32). Storm De Hirsch and Harry Smith are self-declared magicians. Kenneth Anger, best-known of the fringe film makers, regards Aleister Crowley as one of his heroes and has filmed the entire set of erotic paintings in Crowley's Abbey of Thelema in Sicily. Anger says, 'I have always considered movies evil; the day that cinema was invented was a black day for mankind ... So I consider myself as working Evil in an evil medium' (Sitney, 1974, p.133).

The films often reflect the esoteric interests of their makers, with themes taken from Hindu mythology, Siberian shamanism, witchcraft, satanism and sex magic. Much footage is devoted to rituals from the Tibetan *Book of the Dead*, from the pre-Buddhist Bon religion of Central Asia, and from Tantrism. The accompanying music may be microtinal or atonal, or an improvisation on one of the modal styles of the East.

7.

COMMENT

Interpretation

For centuries tantriks have been at variance about whether the Tantras should be taken in their exact literal sense or given a metaphorical meaning. The fact that the writings are open to alternative interpretations has been emphasized by modern scholars as well. In Tantra, according to Professor H. V. Glasenapp, a learned authority on the subject, 'everything seems to mean everything at some time or the other'.

From the beginning some tantriks have maintained that their philosophy is subject to understanding and evaluation at more than one level, and have condemned those who, failing to comprehend the figurative message of the text, plunge into the chakrapuja rites for mere sensual gratification. Such foolhardy people will be relegated after death to a dreadful hell reserved for those who kill a priest, revile the virtuous, or destroy an embryo. And in this hell they will remain till the dissolution of the universe.

In this view, a high moral character is required of the tantrik. According to the *Gautamiya Tantra*, the practitioner should have overcome passion, and should be virtuous and self controlled. Undertaking the five makaras, warns the *Kularnava Tantra*, is more difficult than walking on sword blades, riding a tiger, or holding a poisonous snake. It further states, that if religion consisted of the mere enjoyment of wine and women, then drunkenness and debauchery would be esteemed religious virtues. The *Gandharva Tantra* warns that anyone performing the rites in a profane way without understanding will be doomed to eternal damnation.

On the other hand, many tantriks insist on a literal interpretation of their scriptures. In their view the Tantras assert the

importance of the senses being brought into fullest operation
during the rites. Tantrik adepts of the Kaula school, for
example, resist all attempts to allegorize or spiritualize the
content, affirming that a literal interpretation is the only one
intended by the writers. Any changes on the grounds of
symbolism would render the text and teaching quite valueless.

Most modern exponents agree that to put a symbolic interpretation on texts of such obvious meaning, in order to avoid their
more unsavoury implications, or because they shock the
sensibilities of the prude, would require considerable scholastic
ingenuity. The writings are often so explicit that it would be
stretching one's imagination too far to read them in any other
way. To interpret the many clear references to the phallus,
vulva, semen, ejaculation, adultery, incest, in terms of divinity,
soul, enlightenment or salvation, is simply to deny that words
have any meaning at all.

When Western scholars first began translating the texts and
describing the rituals, they often either refrained from doing so
in any detail, or gave an alternative rendering of the words,
excusing their reticence on the grounds that certain passages
were too indelicate to be set down in writing. Even in our own
time scholars have felt uneasy about the nature of some of the
material they have had to interpret.

Sir John Woodroffe, for instance, who translated many
tantrik works, gave a considerably 'watered down rendering' of
some of the verses, presumably because the subject-matter
embarrassed him. Giuseppe Tucci in *Tibetan Painted Scrolls*
considered certain tantrik rites too crude to be fully described;
and David Snellgrove, editor of the *Hevajra Tantra*, admitted
that some passages in his translation had been toned down or
left out altogether.

Yoga

It would be useful at the present stage to review the main
features of Tantrism in practice, and to consider them in the
light of recent criticism, eastern and western. To do so, it
becomes necessary to broaden the basis of the subject and touch
on elements that are not strictly tantrik.

To begin with, it should be borne in mind that the orthodox
Hindu regards Tantrism as being opposed to the Vedas, the

sacred scriptures of the Hindu religion. In Tantrism, an essential part of preparatory training involves yoga; and hatha yoga, which lays down the principles, has no Vedic sanction. What popularly passes for yoga in the West is a system of simple physical exercises requiring persistence, practice, patience and concentration.

The yoga-stricken Western aspirant who disdains the usual courses of physical culture provided in his own part of the world may derive some psychological benefit from operating under the banner of a 'magical' Eastern system that promises wonderful results; but in the end he will obtain from it no greater benefit than he would from any sensible régime of physical training. The long life and superabundant vitality of the yogi adept is one of the most widespread delusions. Respiratory and cardiac disease, and ailments affecting the head, eyes, ears, nose, stomach, kidneys, spine and genitals, are extremely common among Eastern yogis, even of advanced grade.

Certain breathing exercises recommended in hatha yoga can be injurious, even when practised under competent supervision. Continued rapid breathing for long periods, retention of breath beyond normal endurance, alteration of the natural breathing rhythm, may all produce alarming symptoms. These exercises can enlarge the alveoli or air cells, making them lose their elasticity; cause the normal breathing reflexes to go out of gear so that the neophyte may end up having to struggle for breath like an asthmatic; they can affect the heart rate and blood pressure; alter the oxygen, carbon dioxide, acid, alkali, lactate and calcium content of the blood; affect the efficiency of the brain. They may also cause buzzing sensations in the head, blackouts, as well as muscular incoordination, emotional instability, loss of judgment and hallucinatory states.

Most of the asanas, on which so much emphasis is frequently laid, are not exercises but static meditative postures. The most common is the seated *siddha-asana*, the simple cross-legged posture, with one heel firmly pressed against the perineum. To begin with such heel pressure causes a mild erection, which in time weakens the male organ and may lead to impotence. As its name implies it is the posture of 'attainment' and is the one most often used by ascetics. Another common asana, the headstand, flushes the head, dilates the capilaries of the face, and causes premature sagging of the facial muscles.

Patanjali, the great authority on yoga, desired little more than that an asana should be *sthira-sukham*, 'firm and agreeable', and the best exponents still hold that only that posture is to be sought in which a man can sit longest without discomfort. The weird contortions that make up the gallery of the other asanas are merely frills. There is no evidence to support the notion that any unusual powers accrue through their practice. Many such asanas, misguidedly practised to increase sexual vigour, may well permanently undermine it, as practitioners have learned to their cost. Others affect the muscular balance of the pelvis, and weaken the process that triggers erection.

These outlandish postures are aberrations and have no place in the early texts on yoga. They have been contrived and added on over the centuries, on fanciful analogies with the birds, animals and objects whose qualities they are supposed to confer when the asana position is assumed. They are the work of 'deluded men who mislead the honest seeker'. Some indeed strongly resemble the bizarre stances assumed by patients in hysteric trance, or by schizophrenics in catatonic stupor.

Also part of the yoga régime are exercises designed to control the autonomic nervous system. This involves the extension of conscious control over bodily functions otherwise regulated automatically, such as breathing, body temperature, ejaculation, pulse rate, blood circulation, digestion. Such suspension of the autonomic processes can be obtained by elementary autogenic training that has nothing to do with yoga, and has been achieved by wonder-workers in other parts of the world. Unless carried out under expert guidance, autogenic exercises can be dangerous and cause serious dysfunction of the normal guidance system. In attempting to control consciously what is regulated unconsciously, the aspirant may cause the autonomic system to let go, and it then becomes very difficult to get the natural process to take over again.

Serious doubts have likewise been raised about many other features of yoga training. Staring at the sun; or focusing the eyes on the space between the eyeballs or the tip of the nose for hours on end, can strain and damage the optic nerves and muscles. Repeated exercises for cleaning out the stomach by swallowing a large quantity of water and then regurgitating it, can injure the mucus membranes, impair the secretion of the gastric juices, weaken the digestive system and lead to general debility. Cleansing the nose by sniffing up water alternately through each nostril until the water flows out of the mouth; or passing a piece of soft string up into one nostril and out through the mouth and pulling it back and forth, can do great injury to the nasal blood vessels and inflame the sinuses.

There are other exercises which become progressively more and more extreme, and only a few need be mentioned here. Thus, a piece of metal bent at one end may be inserted into the mouth and the palate ridge hooked and gently drawn forward. After a few weeks the membrane becomes so flexible that, according to the yogic textbooks, it becomes possible to touch the teeth with the soft palate. The frenum (the thin membrane) under the tongue may be cut so that the tongue can be rolled up and back into the gullet. This is done to prevent the 'leakage' of the vitalic fluid that drips from the sahasrara chakra in the brain, so the yogi can utilize it.

Again, a plug may be inserted into the rectum and the sphincter trained in anal contractions so that water may be drawn up through the rectum. Or a metal tube inserted into the urethral canal and the penis trained in rhythmic contractions so that water may be drawn into the bladder. Such rectal and penial contraction exercises are essential if the tantrik is to be competent in the *oli* techniques already described, which enable him to vampirize on the vitalic energies of the female during intercourse.

All these procedures, as experts on the subject constantly point out, are quite futile. Nothing worthwhile is achieved by tampering with the body in this manner. The harmful effects, on the other hand, hardly need stressing. Often the internal organs are infected, become swollen and painful, lose their natural vigour, and are damaged beyond repair.

The *Gheranda Samhita* (c. 1350), written by a yogi practitioner, cautions against the risk of serious disease through the wrongful practice of yoga. The *Hatha-yoga Pradipika* by Svatmarama Svamin (fl. 1430) states that the practitioner will be killed if the exercises are not properly carried out. Later authorities have continued in the same vein. Ramakrishna (d. 1886) would have nothing to do with hatha yoga and all its unnatural posturing, for, he said, you cannot forget your body if you spend your time twisting it about. In any case he regarded all such practices with abhorrence.

Enthusiasts who believe hatha yoga has any hidden advantages over other methods of self-development may note the words of Dr Theos Bernard, who studied under various gurus in India and achieved remarkable success in hatha yoga, which he practised for many years: 'I have found that it holds no magic, performs no miracles, and reveals nothing supernatural'.

At the same time, knowledgeable exponents East and West have repeatedly sounded a note of warning relating to certain intrinsic dangers arising from the practice of yoga. These dangers, it is said, are not only physical but psychic, since a magical and occult bias tinges all levels and systems of yoga. What might appear a superficial dabbling with pranayama and the asanas, may turn out to be the first step along a path of occultism beset with potential hazards for the unsuspecting.

The physical exercises of yoga are specifically designed to prepare the body for the psycho-spiritual changes that are to come. Down the ages yoga has been used first and foremost as a vestibule leading to the inner sanctuary of occult experience. The yoga scholar and Sanskrit authority R. S. Mishra writes, 'Behind every psychic investigation, behind mysticism, occultism, etc., knowingly or unknowingly, the yoga system is present'. Writing in her *Secret Doctrine* about these aspects of tantrik and hatha yoga occultism, Madame Blavatsky, who had considerable knowledge of the subject, says that 'nothing but harm' can come to those who practice it. She goes on to emphasize in her own fashion, 'I would strongly dissuade any student from attempting any of these hatha yoga practices, for he will ruin himself entirely. Beware, I say.'

Similar conclusions are reached by many other researchers. Shaw Desmond, a student and practitioner with many years close experience says, 'The psychic pitfalls of yoga are more numerous than all the others together'. Ernest Wood, author of several books on yoga, believes all forms of hatha yoga to be 'extremely dangerous', adding that many have brought upon themselves serious bodily disorder, incurable illness and even madness by practising them without proper conditions of body and mind. As Hans Rieker puts it, yoga is not something to be trifled with if we consider that any misunderstanding in the practice can mean death or insanity. Agehnanda Bharati, Austrian-born Hindu convert and tantrik authority, states that he knows over a dozen cases where people have developed psychopathological symptoms following the yoga path of some of its modern exponents.

Many Indian masters endorse these views. Commenting on yoga exercises, asanas, and breathing techniques, a recent oberver, Shree Purohit Swami, writes, 'In India and Europe I came across three hundred people who suffered permanently from wrong practices, and doctors on examination found that there was nothing organically wrong and consequently could not prescribe'. Swami Prabhavananda lists brain injury, incurable disease and insanity as potential hazards of wrong yoga practice. According to one of today's foremost Indian exponents of yoga, Gopi Krishna, it is commonly known in India that hatha yoga can lead to insanity (Wilson and Weldon, 1980, p.74). Swami Chidananda of the Sivananda ashram, another expert in the field, speaking of hatha yoga, warns that 'it is like trying to play with fire' (Caycedo, 1966, p.56).

Chakras

In considering tantrik esoteric physiology a considerable discrepancy will be found to exist in the different accounts of the chakras as outlined in the various Hindu and Buddhist texts. They are neither consistently named, nor listed or described. In number they range between four and twelve.

A modern tantrik of the west, Kenneth Grant, points out that the sounds and shapes associated with each chakra as given in the textbooks on yoga are misleading, and it is unlikely that any two 'maps' of the chakras would tally. They will vary according to the temperamental disposition and spiritual development of the practitioner. This only serves to underline the essentially subjective nature of the chakra experience. Grant indeed suggest that the chakras come into existence only when the kundalini is active.

If there is confusion about the number, location and description of the chakras, there is even more confusion about the kundalini, the methods of its arousal, the manner and limits of its ascent, and even its very existence. Some experts dismiss the upward journey as fanciful. The idea of the kundalini travelling from its hiding place near the human anus for a secret tryst with Shiva in the cerebrum is, according to Agehananda Bharati, 'latter-day nonsense'.

The kundalini fire-force is a largely Hindu concept, and plays little part in Buddhist esotericism. Sierksma says that the Buddhist mystic 'is not interested in the slightest to know where the various "lotus centres" are located'. He simply 'makes' these centres (1966, p.192). And from certain accounts of its arousal and ascent it would seem that the kundalini may in fact be a purely imaginary force created by concentration.

Gopi Krishna, a contemporary exponent of kundalini yoga, has had personal experience of this force, with all the usual mysterious accompaniments: strange sensations at the base of the spine; tingling feelings at the root of the sexual organs; sounds like the roar of a waterfall; a stream of liquid light suffusing the brain; being immersed in a sea of luminescence. He had been practising daily meditation since his teens and it was only when he was thirty-four years old that he had this experience. He had spent several hours every day concentrating on the chakras, contemplating an imaginary lotus in full bloom radiating light in all directions. Small wonder then, the psychologist would say, that after eighteen years of single-minded concentration on these images, he should experience the kundalini.

Ramakrishna, the modern Hindu saint, tells how he once decided to worship the god Rama in the form of the monkey-devotee Hanuman. To assist him in his devotions he behaved like Hanuman, ate only fruit and nuts, spent a great deal of time perched on trees. 'And the most marvellous thing', he says, 'was that the lower end of my spine lengthtened nearly an inch'. When he stopped practising this form of devotion it resumed its normal size (Menen, 1974, p.131). Whether the miniature tail was an actual objective phenomen, or a purely subjective illusion, it does indicate the formative power of the psyche.

It is noteworthy also, that the kundalini, which looms so large in tantrik forms of yoga, is not even mentioned in many other systems. In Mookerjee's asessment the tantrik knows that 'by meditating on anything as the self, one becomes that thing', and, he concludes, 'This is the way to awaken the coiled-up

energy, kundalini' (1972, p.12). The power of the mind creates
the illusion of the chakra vortices and of the kundalini, and then
by continued meditation the whole exercise of the arousal and
ascent is brought into operation.

The discrepant accounts of the chakras have been explained
by some authorities on the ground that 'we are dealing with
impalpable inner experience', and this again would appear to
confirm the subjective nature of the chakras. Patanjali in the
fifth century called the kundalini 'imaginary'. Agehananda
Bharati, a present-day tantrik authority says, 'kundalini is a lot
of claptrap'.

Although the tendency of some modern critics is to treat the
whole mythology of the chakras, with their lotus petals radiating
coloured lights, as entirely illusory, the chakras have been made
the subject of unbiased scientific study. They are thought to
correspond to certain parts of the physiological system known
to medical science.

The theory was first put into appropriate medical terms by
Major B. D. Basu of the Indian medical service, who, in an essay
published in *Guy's Hospital Gazette* in 1889, equated the chakras
with various plexuses. More recent scholars, like H. Jacobs,
have asociated them with the endocrine glands, with certain
ganglia or bundles of nerve fibre, and with knots of connective
tissue within the human anatomy.

The ancient Greeks, Chinese, Tibetans, the Jewish Kabalists,
and medieval Hesychast monks, among others, also recognized
the existence of certain focal areas within the human body that
governed its vital physiological and mental processes. These
were believed to be situated in the following locations: the head,
governing thought and sensation; the throat, governing speech,
the carotid artery and the jugular vein, as well as mental and
physical well-being; the heart, governing breathing; the navel,
governing the emotions; the sex organs, governing the generative functions; the rectum, governing excretion.

No magical element was attached to these areas, but it was
regarded as important to keep them under control, and this was
usually done by concentrating on one or the other when needed.
Because of the stimulating effect of focusing one's attention on
the lower centres, they were seldom mentioned, and if mentioned
were not made the object of meditation.

The sufis spoke of these centres as *lataif* (singular, *latifa*), but were concerned with no centres below the navel. The eleventh century Hesychast monks of Greece, named the two lower centres, the sex organs and anal sphincter, but did not use them in their prayer rhythms as it was thought to be inimical to the spirit of religious contemplation.

Several Buddhist schools of meditation, even though tantrik, also name only the four upper centres: head, throat, heart and navel. When the lower centres are referred to it is specifically in order to exclude them from meditative exercises. In Hinduism too, the original chakra system was confined to the four top chakras. The present seven-chakra system is a very recent concept, and cannot be found in any of the early authoritative texts.

As with the other exercises, all responsible exponents of yogic self-development have strong words of caution against any reckless tampering with the chakra system, and especially arousing dormant forces within the body by concentrating on the sexual and anal centres (which are closely interconnected), whether in terms of the kundalini or not. Meditation on these 'psychic centres' as they are sometimes called, will stimulate them and cause them to be needlessly and uncontrollably activated. Such stimulation, by long periods of concentration, leads to sensations of burning heat, and, as already stated, may result in mental breakdown and sudden death.

Swami Vivekananda (d. 1902) strongly opposed the pursuit of psychic powers in this way because they were based on the sexual centres, the arousal of which, he said, results in 'the most terrible pranks'. Another well-known teacher, Swami Chidananda, speaks of the undesirable consequences of awakening the 'lower channels', for the powers released easily get beyond control and the practitioner becomes debauched (Caycedo, 1966, p.66). A Buddhist publication states, 'More men and women have been driven insane through a premature awakening of the forces latent in these centres than most students realize' (Anonymous, 1935, p.23).

Shree Purohit Swami, himself an expert, found he could neither sit nor stand, and went through a condition bordering on madness, as a result of kundalini yoga. Gopi Krishna, probably the foremost exponent in this field today, writes that for many years the experience was 'painful, obsessive, even phantasmic ... for some time I was hovering between sanity and insanity'. He states that wrong practice of this system can cause tormenting pressure on the reproductive organs, and 'an all-consuming sexual thirst that is never assuaged' (1975, p.14). One great drawback, he adds, is that experiments in kundalini yoga can bring about spontaneous and involuntary 'arousal' that the mind cannot cope with. In his view most schizophrenics and manic depressives probably represent a malfunctioning kundalini.

Siddhis
The ultimate objective of all yoga training undertaken by the tantrik is the attainment of siddhis or 'powers', which will enable him to do things beyond the capabilities of the ordinary person.

India has been famed as the land of goety and illusory wonders from earliest times, and in the popular imagination every sort of miraculous feat has been attributed to the Indian sadhu. These include: creating phantasmic illusions of men and things by 'glamour', the rope trick, the mango trick, insensibility to pain, fire-walking, immunity to cold, inedia or non-eating for long periods, feats of materialization and dematerialization, teleportation or the instantaneous transference of things across a distance, burial alive, walking on water, levitation, volitation or flying through the air, bilocation or being in two places at the same time, besides various sexual powers such as lifting a heavy weight tied to the male member by inducing a powerful erection, and more recently, eating nails, needles and razor-blades, and swallowing nitric and sulphuric acid.

Many of these feats have never actually been authenticated, but form part of the 'legendry' of the east. Those that have been witnessed and confirmed are not exclusive to India, and have been performed by Siberian shamans, Fiji Islanders, African magicians, Egyptian fakirs, and allegedly, European witches. Many are part of the stock-in-trade of the common conjurer in all parts of the world and have been done without the aid of yoga, Sanskrit mantras, or dedication to Hindu gods.

Stories of yogis allowing themselves to be buried alive for weeks at a time were apparently confirmed by responsible witnesses until the end of the last century. But when investigated under more rigorous scientific conditions in our own day, the 'weeks' turn out to be no more than two or three hours, in a box containing sufficient oxygen for an individual trained in slow and shallow breathing to remain interred for a marginally longer time than the untrained person.

Control of breathing and heart-rate can be achieved by anyone with practice. With few exceptions the endurance records of most present-day yogis in this respect are far from impressive, and here again, can be duplicated by non-yogis using autogenic methods. In an experiment conducted in March 1970 in Topeka, Kansas, an Indian Yogi, Swami Rama of Rishikesh, stopped his heart from pumping blood for seventeen seconds. Such feats undoubtedly have some physiological interest, but bear no relationship to the fantastic claims of suspended animation made by Indian wonder-workers.

In 1966 an Indian yogi Lakshmanasandra Srikanta Rao announced that he could walk on water and undertook to give a public demonstration of his power. In the presence of 5000 spectators in Bombay, he attempted to walk across a concrete tank filled with water, and promptly sank to the bottom at the first step.

Concerning the sexual siddhis, it has been said that hoisting small weights with the penis can be done with the aid of erethetic drugs. But the more extravagant claims along these lines can only be classed among the fables of the East. Colaabavala, however, says that there are many reliable witnesses who swear to have seen tantrik sadhus pull a bullock cart as much as a furlong with the vehicle tied to the linga. Other sexual powers, such as the ones enabling a man to seduce countless virgins or cohabit with other men's wives, merely call into question the moral value of the siddhis.

In Indian legend generally, the great rishis or sages of old, who were said to be possessed of almost divine powers and were held up as paragons of wisdom, were usually far from benign and serene tempered, as might be expected of those who had attained a state of transcendent bliss. Almost without exception they were irascible in the extreme and turned viciously on anyone who provoked them, sometimes reducing them to ashes with a single glance. The rishi's baleful wrath is a recurrent theme of Hindu mythology.

The supernatural siddhis associated with them, and with their later counterparts, the yogis and sadhus of Hindu tradition, and the dreaded *dragpo* or wrathful siddhis of Tibetan tantrik sorcerers, were concerned principally with maleficia or evil deeds, seeking to harm and hurt, and inspired by destructive rage, malice, envy and hatred. The ancient siddhas projected hostile currents to cause calamity and disease, bring down hail and storm, blight the crops and make cattle die. If they possessed the power to bless they showed little or no evidence of it. Their curses crippled and blinded, caused sterility and insanity. They could render a man impotent or a woman barren, and kill a child in its mother's womb. By their spells they 'knotted up' the larger and lesser ducts of the victim's body so that he was unable to perform his natural functions and died an agonizing death.

Many of India's great thinkers were aware that siddhis may well corrupt the individual who possesses them, and pursuit of them was regarded as derogating from the highest spiritual ideals. Buddha decried the thirst for siddhis. When he once met a yogi who proudly announced that after many years of effort he could now walk across the river, the Buddha replied, 'What a pity to have spent so much effort; a little further on they will take you across for a penny'. He said to his disciple Kevaddha, 'It is because I see the danger of performing occult marvels [siddhis] that I execrate and abominate them'.

The philosopher Patanjali, who wrote the classic work on yoga, condemned the pursuit of siddhis as 'an impediment to the attainment of the highest truth'. Ramakrishna deplored the pursuit of siddhis as foolish and vain, saying emphatically that they should be 'shunned like filthy excrement'. His disciple Vivekananda likewise warned against striving for such sorcerous powers and stressed the need for totally avoiding them. Despite the long-standing tradition of siddhis in Tibet, the teachings of the ruling Gelug-pa sect of Tibetan Buddhism also condemn all demonstrations of occult phenomena and hankering after supernatural siddhis. Both the Dalai Lama and the Panchen Lama affirm that siddhis have no place in Tibetan Buddhism.

Mantras
The importance of the mantra is emphasized in all tantrik

exercises. No ritual is complete unless accompanied by the appropriate set of magical sounds, syllables, words or verses. but no unanimity exists about the use of any particular mantra, about its purpose, its meaning, its correct pronunciation, or the occasions for which it is apposite or effective.

These sounds are said to have mysterious meanings. But the interpretation of a mantra is no simple matter, and no two exponents will explain a single mantra in the same way. There are mantra-dictionaries *(mantra-koshas)* that list and interpret mantras, but again no two dictionaries give the same meaning for any mantra.

In some schools of yogic practice, the mantras recommended include certain sets of rhyming or con-sonant sounds that have to be repeated hour after hour. For example: gang, ging, goong, gaing, goung; vang, ving, voong, vaing, voung; ksham, kshim, kshoom, kshaim, kshoum; klang, kling, kloong, klaing, kloung; ram, ram, ram; kham, kham, kham. This is reminiscent of a condition known to psychopathology as echolalia, which is a symptom of certain types of mental disorder. The afflicted person is obsessed with sound, and drugs himself with his own endless chanting. It is in effect a form of self-hypnosis, known to cause cerebral intoxication, often leading to delusions and other hallucinatory states.

According to popular belief, many mantras go back to the creative, sustaining or destructive phonemes uttered by the deities themselves in their dealings with the world. A famous swami on a visit to Greenwich Village, New York, discoursing on the antiquity of the magical syllable *om*, told his audience that it was a universal divine sound. In all seriousness he declared that even Jehovah identified himself with the sacred sound, as could be seen from the Bible (Ex. 3.14), when God told Moses, 'I OM that I OM'.

As we have seen, the power attributed to the mantra is extraordinary. In Indian legend, everything one can conceive of may be achieved simply to intoning the right mantra, and belief in their efficacy is as widespread as ever. Today, post-graduate studies in mantra-power are being conducted at the Khapri Institute near Nagpur in India to see whether there is any crop improvement in fields irrigated by mantra-magnetized water.

Mantra experts make a great thing about the importance of

enunciating the mantra in the proper way. Wrongly pronounced, the mantra will have no effect at all, or what is worse, may have an effect opposite to the one described. This view however, is not shared by all. Lama Anagarika Govinda points out that mantras in Tibet, even those derived from India, are not pronounced as they would be in India, and yet are regarded as equally effective. As any student of Sanskrit knows, the pronunciation of Sanskrit, even among pundits, may vary from one part of India to another. Again, Western students who learn the mantras pronounce them as best they can, and often not as they should be pronounced.

Writing at the beginning of the present century, M. N. Dutt observes that the giving of mantras 'has become a trade in our country' (1979, p.29). But the mystique of the mantra was the butt of caustic comment from pre-Buddhist times. Charvaka, a non-Aryan sage mentioned in the *Mahabharata*, castigated the mantra-mongers as scoundrels and tricksters. The Jains too had some harsh things to say both to the mantra-men and their dupes.

Buddha, while not opposed to repeating verses as an aid to remembrance, repeatedly warned against the folly of trusting in the efficacy of mantras. The Hinayana Buddhists had little time for those who peddled their spells and incantations to provide salvation and enlightenment. In colloquial Sinhalese, the vernacular of modern Sri Lanka (akin to Pali the language of ancient Buddhism), the word mantra means something like hocus-pocus.

Meditation

Another essential feature of Tantrism is meditation, which is very much part of the Hindu and Buddhist mystical system. If a mantra establishes a magical link, meditation reaffirms and strengthens it. In tantra one of a number of objects is suggested for the student's meditation. These objects vary considerably. Thus, one may survey the thirty-two parts of the body; or direct the mind to the 'contemplation of corpses in various degrees of decomposition' (Conze, 1980, p.25). One might concentrate on one or more of the chakras, or on one's phallus. One could concentrate on the yoni of a woman one desires to attract. For this purpose she should be imagined standing before the tantrik, completely nude, red in colour, her body bound, her neck in a noose, her heart pierced with a hook, and over her pudenda is to be visualized a blazing mandala or diagram which must be made the object of intense concentration, preferably while intoning a mantra.

One object of meditation often recommended by the guru, is the guru himself. Dwelling on the 'godship' of the guru during contemplation brings great spiritual merit, especially when accompanied by mantras of praise and adoration. Later we shall consider the further implications of such guruolatry.

Great psychological benefits have been claimed on behalf of meditation, especially the kind known as Transcendental Meditation (see below). Medical researchers today have measured the physiological reactions of a person during meditative trance and have found that it produces many beneficial effects. These include: a lowered metabolic rate; a fall in oxygen consumption, in carbon dioxide elimination, in cardiac output, in heart-rate and respiratory rate, and in the lactate concentration in the blood (showing that tension is lowered). GSR (galvanic skin response) or skin resistance to mild electric current is increased (skin resistance decreases when stress is present), and there is also an increase in slow alpha rhythms of the brain.

But, as already pointed out, all these signs, which indicate a lessening of tension, worry, stress and anxiety, are not unique to Hindu or Buddhist meditative methods, but follow any period of relaxation, quiet contemplation, prayerfulness, tranquillity and peaceful solitude, especially if regularly carried out.

Here again we find that the religious tradition in general is wary of meditative methods. Powerful undercurrents can easily be generated by mental practices. Buddha laid considerable emphasis on how one's mental powers should be directed, the methods to be used, and their object and purpose. Not just any meditation. Not wrongful meditation. Not mischievous, harmful, selfish or licentious meditation. Of the 'Eight Paths' that underlie and constitute the whole of Buddha's teachings, one path was concerned solely with what Buddha called 'right meditation'.

The quietistic devotions, prayers and contemplations of monotheistic religions such as Judaism, Christianity and Islam are not meditation in the Indian sense of the term. It has long

been understood that the euphoria that sometimes results from
meditation is an amoral quality, to which good or evil may be
attached, depending on what is made to fill the receptive mind.
These religious systems recognize the pitfalls that lie in the path
when such a profound and personal exercise as meditation is
dissociated from a high spiritual motivation; hence no method
of inner development is undertaken in a spirit of self-sufficiency.
In essence, meditation is a humble approach to God as a
creature to his Creator in the form of prayer.

Alice Bailey, a well-known occultist with great experience in
these matters, wrote: 'It is essential to realize that meditation
can be very dangerous work'. Sri Krishna Prem says that unless
one has the proper control, 'it is safer to play with dynamite than
to practice the yoga of meditation'. There are probably few
serious writers on Eastern occultism who have not received
their share of letters from desperate people asking for help in a
situation created as a result of foolhardy dabbling in yoga,
meditation and tantrik ritualism.

The Maharishi
One of the chief contemporary exponents of meditation and
mantra-power is J. N. Srivastava (born 1918), better known as
Maharishi Mahesh Yogi, who for some years past has been
selling an occult system of self-development called Transcendental Meditation (TM). The endorsement given to his
system by certain celebrities in the entertainment field caused
an epidemic of conversions in the western world. Thousands of
people swore that TM-sidhi practice had helped them to give up
bad habits, lose weight, improve their sex lives and earn more
money.

According to the Maharishi, arduous discipline and long bouts
of concentration are a waste of time. All one has to do is sit
comfortably for a few minutes every day and mentally repeat a
certain mantra in a kind of relaxed trance. The mantra issued in
TM consists of two or three syllables and costs about £30, and all
are variations of a few basic sounds, usually with the reverberating
m, *n* or *ng* component. In each case the mantra is said to vibrate in
consonance with the pupil's personal rhythm, helping him to
rise to the 'fourth state of consciousness', or 'transcendental
state of being'.

Still more advanced is the Maharishi's SCI (Science of Creative Intelligence), which works on a deeper psychic level and promises greater powers. In a so-called 'flying room' in one of the European TM ashrams, students are said to levitate, but they do not give demonstrations. Special mattresses can be purchased by pupils who wish to practise levitation.

Some of those who have studied the subject state that what is offered in TM as a means of attaining tranquillity unconnected with any religious ties actually involves a profound change of spiritual direction on the part of the pupil. They state that while purporting to be non-religious, TM is a scarcely disguised form of supernaturalism based on the occult properties of the Sanskrit phoneme.

It is no small matter to ask of an initiate that he meditate for twenty minutes twice every day on a mantra, which is not an innocuous sound but is specifically designed to work its magic in the chela's deep unconscious. The meaning of the mantra is unknown to him, and he is told not to disclose it to anyone, but he must be prepared to hold it in his mind for some forty minutes every day. In plain words, he must accept its talismanic virtues as an act of blind faith.

The Maharishi says, 'We do something here according to Vedic rites, particular specific chanting to produce an effect in some other world, draw the attention of those higher beings or gods living there' (Wilson and Weldon, 1980, p.49). This would imply that TM is inextricably bound up with the Hindu pantheon, a fact which may not be in accord with the religious sentiments of those brought up in a monotheistic faith. The Maharishi has inaugurated the Age of Enlightenment, has set up ashrams in several places around the world, and envisages a world-wide spiritual empire on Vedic lines (see Snehi and Saxena, 1981). Among the members of the imperial cabinet is a Minister of Immortality.

From various accounts it would seem that far from achieving equilibrium, many TM students suffer adverse psychological effects: uncontrollable nervous tension, anxiety and depression – precisely those symptoms that TM is supposed to alleviate. Some have complained of headaches of unusual severity, and blackouts. A few reported more serious symptoms: noises in the head, strange voices, hallucinations, epileptic fits and complete

mental breakdown, forcing them to seek psychiatric care. Some
of these findings were publicized in a London television docu-
mentary on 31 May 1981.

TM instructors and students who have entered more deeply
into the cult often become disturbed at having unwittingly
entered into a quasi-mystical experience antithetic to their
beliefs. According to researcher John White, in Transcendental
Meditation the altar-picture of the Maharishi is combined with
the mantra, to 'finish the job of desensitizing the mind to all
alien thought systems and of transplanting the mind from one
cultural system to another'. The pledge signed by every TM
teacher includes an obligation to 'serve the holy tradition',
which some might regard as a form of guruolatry. The TM
initiation ceremony contains a reference to 'Guru in the glory of
Brahman. Guru in the glory of Vishnu' (Wilson and Weldon,
1980, p.36).

Many cult members find they are unable to come to terms
with the change they are required to make from one faith, or
even no faith, to a strange system whose metaphysical com-
plexities they can barely comprehend. The readjustment, and
the wrenching shift of loyalties can apparently have very
unpleasant consequences. The suicide rate among TM teachers
in the US is said to be appreciably higher than the national
average. A former TM instructor, Kathy Filler says, 'The ones
that don't kill themselves either get really weird or eventually
drop back into drugs or just fall apart (Wilson and Weldon,
1980, p.40).

These may be extreme cases, but in the light of more general
criticism too, it is obviously desirable to bear in mind the words
of caution expressed by knowledgeable people regarding the
adoption (without a proper understanding of its implications) of
any esoteric practice, whatever its alleged merits.

The Bhagwan
Another remarkable phenomenon among today's cult leaders is
Rajneesh Chandra Mohan, born in 1931 of Jain parents. He
made a study of philosophy and comparative religion, received
'total enlightenment' at the age of twenty-one while sitting
under a tree (Annett, 1976, p.60), and became a guru without
initiation from another guru, assuming the title, first of *Acharya*,

or 'teacher', and then *Bhagwan*, or 'divine one'.

More than any other guru in India, Bhagwan Shree Rajneesh, a self-declared tantrik, is well acquainted with recent philosophical developments in the West, and familiar with the clichés of contemporary psychology. A polymath, he has written on Buddha, Tao, Tantra, Yoga, Vedanta, Jesus, Zen, Kabir, the Baul mystics, the Sufis, Heraclitus and others, over 100 volumes in all, consisting largely of his personal comments. Perhaps inspired by the literary avant-garde of a few decades ago, he has also produced a Rajneesh Nothing Book, made up of 200 blank pages.

His darshan addresses and the work sessions at his ashram in Pune (formerly Poona) represent a medly of different systems: the bioenergetics of Wilhelm Reich; the teachings of the eighteenth-century Jewish Hasids; the *latihan* of the Subud movement of the Indonesian mystic Muhammad Subuh; George Gurdjieff's harmonious development; Arthur Janov's primal therapy; the rebirthing of Leonard Orr; the rolfing of Ida Rolf; Werner Erhart's est; Randolf Stone's polarity balancing; the mind dynamics of Alexander Everett; the sensitivity training of David Viscott; the kinesiotherapy of Frederick Matthias Alexander. His disciples practise sufi dancing, shiatzu massage, dervish whirling, karate, t'ai chi (slow motion exercises), asanas, pranayama, kundalini, yoga, meditation, and nude sexual 'encounters'.

Rajneesh dismisses the Maharishi's TM as being 'good for sleep, not for meditation'. But he recognizes that meditation can be employed as a means of 'deconditioning' and 'unlearning', and his own meditation system and lectures constitute, in their own way, a psychologically unsettling régime during which his pupils undergo a virtual conversion process. The discipline is not complete until the lay candidate has become a *sannya* or religious disciple. The term *ma* is sometimes used for the female disciple.

Initiates drop their own names and are given Hindu names, so that Peter and Mary may find themselves re-named Govind and Lakshmi. The Bhagwan rubs their forehead to transfer energy and 'open the third eye', and then presents them with a rebirth certificate. Thereafter, the sannyas wear orange robes as a final token of having joined a new holy order, with allegience that to

all appearances seems to be directed to the person of the
Bhagwan himself.

There can be little doubt about the influence Rajneesh has on
some of his devotees. Shannon Jo Ryan, daughter of US
congressman Leo Ryan who was killed in Guyana in November
1978 by the adherents of cult leader Jim Jones, has become a
follower of the Bhagwan. She stated that she did not think a
suicide situation like Jonestown would arise in the ashram, as
the two movements were utterly different, but some devotees of
the guru had said they would be prepared to kill themselves or
others if he so demanded.

Rajneesh has taken on the mantle, and more, of the great
ones of the past. To his disciples he is today's Buddha, Christ,
Lao Tzu. 'Those who have loved Jesus', he says, 'will see Jesus in
me; if they have loved Buddha, they will see Buddha in me; if
they have loved Muhammad, they will see Muhammad in me'.
Referring to Christianity he remarks, 'All through the ages, all
kinds of pathological people have gathered around Jesus'. He
purports to reveal not the Jesus of Christianity, but Jesus seen in
a new light, such as only another Christ, Rajneesh himself, can
see him. He declares in Christ-like terms: 'I am the Truth. I am
the Door. I am the Gate. Come to me. Pass through me.'

Rajneesh has proclaimed himself a god, but in the Indian
context such a claim is not unusual. Blown-up photographs of
him hang from the ashram walls, and countless photographs
adorn the jackets and chapter-heads of his books. There is a
picture of him on the locket of every necklace the faithful are
obliged to wear. 'If you are afraid', the Bhagwan tells them, 'hold
the locket in your hand; I will be there to protect you'. Cynics
have commented that some sannyas perhaps take too literally
the injunction posted at the ashram entrance: 'Shoes and minds
should be left at the gate'.

In his syncretic cult there is nothing that is uniquely of
Rajneesh's minting. What is novel is the role sexuality plays in
it, both in principle and in practice. Rajneesh is the chief
exponent of the divinization of the libido. In keeping with his
tantrik affiliation he tells his sannyas and mas to 'use everything'
including the sexual drive. All inhibitions and taboos are to be
cast off. His call is: 'Approach the sexual act as if you were
entering a temple; and perform it as if it were a prayer'.

In certain assemblies the sannyas may be told to strip completely naked, and they work up in graduated sessions to a climax reminiscent of the orgiastic abandon of the maenads and satyrs at the ancient Greek bacchanalia. It is reported that in Pune the disciples were offered sterilization and vasectomy (Kagal, 1981, p.6), presumably for a more complete and trouble-free liberation. Life in the ashram has been described as 'living in a state of orgasm', as promised by the Tantras in a tantrik heaven. One devotee, Ma Satya Bharti, in a composite picture drawn from the experiences of thirteen inmates, gives a vivid account (1980) of the goings-on at these meetings.

At the beginning of a session there may be a period of auto-touching and exchange-touching, mutual caressing, massaging and tickling. As the tension builds up, the room is filled with the sounds of people making love, men and women, men and men, women and women, coming together, moving from partner to partner, couples and threesomes, sliding over one another's bodies, or entwined in sexual intercourse. Ma Satya Bharti describes one such occasion: 'People in groups, about sixty of them, were lying on the floor naked, with blindfolds on, screwing'.

The immediate effects of this path to emancipation are described in terms of twitching, tremoring, primaling (from primal therapy), catharting (from catharsis), groaning, crying, yelling, wailing, screaming obscenities. There is head-banging, fighting and other forms of violence, grunting, snarling, growling and roaring. The body shakes like a riveting machine, high voltage charges seem to rock the frame, and one feels ready to explode. That near-psychotic conditions are reached is indicated by Ma Satya Bharti's references to epileptic-like fits, possession, and mass hysteria. The whole scene is described as one of pandemonium, and is compared to a madhouse.

Rajneesh claims to be creating a 'Buddhafield', in which obsessions with the ego are cast aside. 'You are fortunate', he announces, 'You are at the beginning of a tradition that is being created here, at the very source. I am creating it.' But in June 1981, the Indian movement received a considerable setback when the Pune ashram was suddenly abandoned by the Bhagwan, who departed without warning for the United States, leaving his Pune followers leaderless and bewildered. He is said to be setting up a huge new centre in Oregon, which is planned to be a 'major experiment in spiritual communism'.

An objective appraisal of Rajneesh's teachings has yet to be made. Present estimates of him are either ludicrously sycophantic or savagely hostile. Those who have dipped into some of his 100-odd volumes might feel that what he has to say sometimes makes good sense, but his critics point out that this is bound to be true of the observations of anyone who is allowed to pontificate unchecked for any length of time.

While in India Rajneesh had never gone out of his way to endear himself to his opponents, who blamed him for what was happening both within and beyond the aegis of the Pune Buddhafield (see Kagal, 1981, p.6). Even those sympathetic to him felt that his tendency to disburse instant wisdom on all subjects and to pass outspoken comments on prominent personalities was not calculated to win friends. It was evident also that his persuasive doctrines and his moral philosophy were wide open to misinterpretation and abuse. Indeed, these proved heady wine to many of his followers. Thus, what might have been designed by the Bhagwan as *orgia* in the Greek sense of mystery rites (to take a charitable view of his sexual mysticism), turned out in practice to be more like group sessions of common or barnyard copulation.

Guruism
An intrinsic feature of every Indian cult is the central part played by the personality of the guru. The eminent Indian scholar and statesman, Sardar K. M. Panikkar wrote, 'There have always been at least 500 living gods in India'. While the earlier tendency of many Western observers was to lump them together as frauds and charlatans, a closer understanding has brought the guru phenomenon into better perspective.

In India it is difficult for any man of light and leading to avoid becoming the object of devout adoration. As a result of the uncritical homage they receive, cult leaders are frequently forced into a situation which they are unable to resist. They become, as it were, the victims of their followers. They are set up on pedestals and invested with divine attributes. Not a few succumb to the temptation and exploit it to their advantage. There are genuine teachers, as there are pretenders, and at times it is difficult to distinguish between them.

The devotees, like the gurus whom they follow, cover a broad spectrum of people of all kinds and classes. The faculty of blind faith is not the prerogative of the East. Underneath the thin veneer of occidental rationalism, too, there often lies a profound gullibility to match anything in India. Witnesses who have observed the spectacle cannot fail to be struck by the spell-binding effect produced on a Western audience by the pronouncements of a brown-skinned guru with a foreign accent. And those who believe in the wonder-working powers of the godman who produces Omega watches and Scotch whisky out of thin air are not only wide-eyed villagers from rural India, but often sober and rational visitors from abroad, who would refuse to accept such feats otherwise than as legerdemain if they were performed by a Western magician back home.

'Miracles' apart, many earnest seekers who have savoured the spirituality of the gurus have often been sadly forced to dismiss as reveries and airy nothings their promises of realization and enlightenment. Many gurus are extremely rich and have wide business interests and even political influence, but few find a place in their scheme of things for the poor, the aged and the socially oppressed.

The glorification of the guru is sometimes carried to extravagant lengths. In some sects the followers accord the guru actual divine honours, worship him in person, and buy images of him to worship at home as the deity incarnate. They prostrate themselves before him, wave incense in his presence, lay flowers at his feet, and sing hymns of adoration in his praise. They will eat the remains of the betel leaf after he has chewed and spat it out, and will drink not only the water in which his feet have been washed, but the water with which he has rinsed his mouth. When he breaks wind it is greeted with suitable *shlokas*, or sacred verses (Gangadhar and Misra, 1976, p.17).

Against the background of their spiritual claims, the character and conduct of many of the holy ones and their organizations have naturally come under close scrutiny. The late Dr Kovoor, a well-known Indian exposer of religious skulduggery, cites numerous instances of the unbecoming behaviour of several world-famous gurus, and he is only one of a growing number of such critics. It would appear that if the censure against the holy ones has been harsh, they often have only themselves to thank. The facts brought to light, both by Indian and foreign investigators, have time and again revealed sex scandals, financial frauds and general moral corruption.

Some Indian observers are inclined to excuse the wild claims of the gurus, their verbal incontinence, their platitudinizing, and their exhibitionism as harmless idiosyncrasy, and a colourful part of the Indian scene. But there are others who are more intolerant, and hostile to the whole guru cult. They maintain that it merely serves to inflame the ego of unbalanced individuals and aggravates their delusions of grandeur. In their view most of these men are evangelists of a quasi-Hindu dharma that is a parody of their religion. It is degrading to the image of India and to Hinduism in particular.

The teachings of the great spiritual leaders of India, both on mysticism and metaphysics, have been important landmarks in the history of human thought. These teachings are not given in exchange for payment. The teachers themselves are usually recluses who dislike publicity and disdain self-aggrandisement. They do not perform or promise miracles. Nor do they seek converts. They believe instead that each person should work out his spiritual solutions against the background of his own social, cultural and religious traditions.

BIBLIOGRAPHY

Abhinavagupta. *Tantrasara*, edited, with notes, by M. R. Sastri, Kashmir Government Publications, Srinagar, 1918.

Ahmed, Fatima. 'Rajneesh: All God's Children', *Sunday Standard Magazine*, Bombay, October 19, 1980.

Aiyar, P.S.S. *Evolution of Hindu Moral Ideas*, Calcutta University Press, 1935.

Altekar, A.S. *The Position of Women in Hindu Civilization*, Mangal Ram, Banaras, 1956.

Anand, Mulk Raj. *Kamakala. Some Notes on the Philosophical Basis of Hindu Erotic Sculpture*, Nagel, Geneva and New York, 1958.

Anand, Mulk Raj, and Kramrisch, Stella. *Homage to Khajuraho*, Marg Monographs, Bombay, 1960.

Anand, Mulk Raj, and Mookerjee, Ajit. *Tantra Magic*, Arnold Heinemann, Delhi, 1977.

Angebert, J.M. *The Occult and the Third Reich*, McGraw Hill, New York, 1975.

Annett, Stephen. *The Many Ways of Being*, Abacus, London, 1976.

Anonymous. *Concentration and Meditation. A Manual of Mind Development*, Buddhist Lodge, London, 1935.

Archer, W.G. *The Loves of Krishna*, Allen & Unwin, London, 1957.

Argüelles, José and Miriam. *Mandala*, Shambala, Berkeley, California; Routledge & Kegan Paul, London, 1972.

Arundale, George S. *Kundalini: An Occult Experience*, 2nd ed., Theosophical Publishing House, Adyar, 1962.

Ashe, Geoffrey. *The Ancient Wisdom*, Macmillan, London, 1977.

Auboyer, J. *Khajuraho*, Mouton, The Hague, 1960.

Avalon, Arthur (see under Woodroffe).

Baba, Pagal. *Temple of the Phallic King: The Mind of India*, edited by E. Rice, Simon & Schuster, New York, 1973.

Bader, C. *Women in Ancient India*, Routledge, London, 1930.

Bagchi, Prabodh Chandra (ed.). *Kaula-jnana-nirnaya: and Some Texts of the School of Matsyendranatha*, Calcutta University Press, 1934.

Bagchi, Prabodh Chandra. *Studies in the Tantras*, Calcutta University Press, 1939.

Bagchi, Prabodh Chandra. *Matsyendra Natha*, Calcutta University Press, 1940.

Bailey, Alice. *Letters on Occult Meditation*, Lucis Publishing Co., New York, 1922.

Ballantine, J.R., and Sastri, Govind. *Yoga Sutras of Patanjali*, Susil Gupta, Calcutta, 1955.

Bancroft, Anne. *Modern Mystics and Sages*, Granada, London, 1978.

Banerjea, A.N. *Philosophy of Gorakhnath*, Raj Press, Gorakhpur, 1962.

Banerjea, Jitendra Nath. *The Development of Hindu Iconography*, Calcutta University Press, 1956.

Banerjea, Jitendra Nath. *Pauranic and Tantrik Religion*, Calcutta University Press, 1966.

Banerji, S.C. *Tantra in Bengal*, Prokash, Calcutta, 1977.

Basu, Manoranjan. *Tantras: A General Study*, Basu Publications, Calcutta, 1976.

Basu, Sri Chandra. *Esoteric Science and Philosophy of the Tantras*, Dharma Press, Allahabad, 1914.

Basu, Sri Chandra. *Shiva Samhita*, Calcutta University Press, 1928.

Baynes, H.G. *Germany Possessed*, Jonathan Capt, London, 1941.

Beal, S. (trans.). *Chinese Accounts of India*, 2 vols., Oxford University Press, 1906.

Belfrage, Sally. *Flowers of Emptiness*, Women's Press, London, 1981.

Bell, Charles. *The Religion of Tibet*, Oxford University Press, 1931.

Bernard, Raymond. *The Serpent Fire*, Health Research, San Francisco, 1959.

Bernard, Raymond. *Agharta: The Subterranean World*, Citadel Press, Secaucus, New Jersey, 1963.

Bernard, Raymond. *The Hollow Earth*, University Books, New York, 1969.

Bernard, Theos. *Hindu Philosophy*, Philosophical Library, New York, 1947.

Bernard, Theos. *Hatha Yoga: The Report of a Personal Experience*, Rider, London, 1950.

Beyer, Stephen. *The Cult of Tara: Magic and Ritual in Tibet*, California University Press, 1973.

Bharati, Agehananda. *The Ochre Robe*, Allen & Unwin, London, 1961.

Bharati, Agehananda. *The Tantrik Tradition*, Rider, London, 1965.

Bharati, Agehananda. *The Light at the Centre*, Ross Erikson, New York, 1976.

Bharti, Ma Satya. *The Ultimate Risk: Encountering Bhagwan Shree Rajneesh*, Wildwood House, London; Bookwise, Sydney, 1980.

Bharti, Ma Satya. *Death Comes Dancing. Celebrating Life with Bhagwan Shree Rajneesh*, Routledge & Kegan Paul, London, 1981.

Bhattacharya, Benoytosh. *Sadhanamala*, 2 vols., Gaekwad Oriental Series, Baroda, 1925, 1928.

Bhattacharya, Benoytosh. *Two Vajrayana Works*, Gaekwad Oriental Series, Baroda, 1929.

Bhattacharya, Benoytosh (ed.). *Jnanasiddhi by Indrabhuti*, Gaekwad Oriental Series, Baroda, 1929.

Bhattacharya, Benoytosh (ed.). *The Guhyasamaja Tantra*, Gaekwad Oriental Series, Baroda, 1931.

Bhattacharya, Benoytosh. *Introduction to Buddhist Esotericism*, Oxford University Press, 1932.

Bhattacharya, Benoytosh. *Shakti-Sangama Tantra*, Gaekwad Oriental Series, Baroda, 3 vols., 1932, 1941, 1947.

Bhattacharya, Benoytosh. *Indian Buddhist Iconography*, Calcutta University Press, 1958.

Bhattacharyya, Narendra Nath. *Indian Mother Goddess*, Indian Studies, Calcutta; Doubleday, New York, 1970.

Bhattacharyya, Narendra Nath. *History of the Sakta Religion*, Manohar, New Delhi, 1974.

Bhattacharyya, Narendra Nath. *History of the Tantrik Religion*, Manohar, New Delhi, 1980.

Blavatsky, H.P. *Isis Unveiled*, Theosophical Publishing Society, London, 1877.

Blavatsky, H.P. *The Secret Doctrine*, Theosophical Publishing Society, London, 3 vols., 1887, 1893, 1897.

Blavatsky, H.P. *Two Books on the Stanzas of Dzyan*, Theosophical Publishing Society, London, 1898.

Blofeld, John. *The Way of Power: A Practical Guide to the Tantrik Mysticism of Tibet*, Allen & Unwin, London; Dutton, New York, 1970.

Blofeld, John. *Beyond the Gods*, Allen & Unwin, London, 1974.

Blofeld, John. *Mantras: Sacred Words of Power*, Allen & Unwin, London, 1979.

Bose, D.N., and Haldar, Hiralal. *Tantras: Their Philosophy and Occult Secrets*, 3rd ed., Oriental Publishing House, Calcutta, 1956.

Bose, Mahindra Mohan. *The Post-Chaitanya Sahaja Cult of Bengal*, Calcutta University Press, 1930.

Botts, Linda (compiler). *Loose Talk: The Book of Quotes from the Rolling Stone Magazine*, Rolling Stone Press, New York, 1980.

Boyd, Doug. *Swami*, Random House, New York, 1976; Rider, London, 1977.

Briggs, George Weston. *Gorakhnath and the Kanphata Yogis*, YMCA Publishing House, Calcutta, 1938; Motilal Banarsidas, Delhi, 1973.

Brennan, J. *The Occult Reich*, Signet, New York, 1974.

Bromage, Bernard. *Tibetan Yoga*, Rider, London; Weiser, New York, 1959.

Brooke, Tal. *The Lord of the Air*, Advent Books, New York, 1978.

Brown, G. W. *The Human Body in the Upanishads*, Standard Printing Works, Jubbulpore, 1921.

Bruce, George. *The Stranglers: The Cult of Thuggee*, Longmans, London, 1968.

Brunton, Paul. *In Search of Secret India*, Rider, London, 1947.

Burton, Sir Richard (trans.). *Ananga Ranga. The Hindu Art of Love*, Kimber, London, 1963; Medical Press, New York, 1964.

Cakravarti, Candra. *Sex Life in Ancient India*, Mukhopadhyay, Calcutta, 1963.

Caycedo, Alfonso. *India of Yogis*, National Publishing House, Delhi, 1966.

Chakraberty, Chandra. *Cultural History of the Hindus*, Vijaya Krishna Bros., Calcutta, 1945.

Chakravarti, Chintaharan. *The Soma or Saura Sects of the Shaivas*, Calcutta University Press, 1932.

Chakravarti, Chintaharan. *The Tantras: Studies on Their Religion and Literature*, Punthi Pustak, Calcutta, 1963.

Chandra, Lokesh. *Mandalas of the Tantra Samucchya*, National Publishing, Delhi, 1969.

Chang, Garma C.C. *Teachings of Tibetan Yoga*, University Books, New York, 1963.

Chang, Garma C.C. *Esoteric Teachings of the Tibetan Tantras*, University Books, New York, 1968.

Chang, Jolan. *The Tao of Love and Sex: The Ancient Chinese Way of Ecstasy*, Wildwood House, London, 1977.

Chapman, Rick M. *How to Choose a Guru*, Harper & Row, New York, 1973; Eel Pie Publishing, London, 1980.

Chattopadhyaya, D. *Lokayata: A Study of Ancient Indian Materialism*, Peoples Publishing House, New Delhi, 1959.

Chattopadhyaya, S. *Reflections on the Tantras*, Motilal Banarsidas, Delhi, 1978.

Chaudhuri, J.B. *The Position of Women in the Vedic Ritual*, Calcutta University Press, 1956.

Chaudhuri, Nirad C. *Hinduism*, Chatto & Windus, London, 1979.

Clark, W.E. *Two Lamaistic Pantheons*, 2 vols., Harvard University Press, 1937.

Cohen, J.M., and Phipps, J.F. *The Common Experience*, Rider, London, 1979.

Colaabavala, F.D. *Tantra: The Erotic Cult*, Orient Paperbacks, New Delhi, 1980.

Colquhoun, Ithell. *Sword of Wisdom: MacGregor Mathers and the Golden Dawn*, Spearman, London, 1975.

Comfort, Alex (ed.) *The Koka Shastra and Other Medieval Indian Writings on Love*, Allen & Unwin, London, 1964.

Conze, Edward. *A Short History of Buddhism*, Allen & Unwin, London, 1980.

Coomaraswamy, Ananda K. *The Dance of Shiva*, Noonday Press, New York, 1957.

Coomaraswamy, Ananda K., and Duggirala, G.K. *Nandikesvara: The Mirror of Gesture*, Wehye, New York, 1936.

Crowley, Aleister. *The Confessions of Aleister Crowley*, edited by J. Symonds and Kenneth Grant, Jonathan Cape, London, 1969.

Curtis, David. *Experimental Cinema*, Dutton, New York; Studio Vista, London, 1971.

Danielli, Mary. *The Anthropology of the Mandala*, Center for Theoretical Biology, Amherst, New York, 1974.

Daniélou, Alain. *Yoga: The Method of Reintegration*, Rider, London, 1951.

Daniélou, Alain. *Hindu Polytheism*, Routledge & Kegan Paul, London; Pantheon, New York, 1964.

Daraul, Arkon. *Secret Societies Yesterday and Today*, Muller, London, 1966.

Dare, Paul. *Indian Underworld: Indian Saints, Sorcerers and Superstitions*, Rider, London, 1938.

Dargyay, Eva. *The Rise of Esoteric Buddhism in Tibet*, Motilal Banarsidas, Delhi, 1977.

Das, S.K. *Sakti or Divine Power*, Central Press, Calcutta, 1934.

Dasgupta, Shashi Bhushan. *Obscure Religious Cults as Background to Bengali Literature*, Calcutta University Press, 1946; ref. ed. Mukhopadhyay, Calcutta, 1962.

Dasgupta, Shashi Bhushan. *An Introduction to Tantrik Buddhism*, Calcutta University Press, 1950; Shambhala, Berkeley, 1974.

Dasgupta, Surendra Nath. *Hindu Mysticism*, Ungar, New York, 1927.

David-Neel, Alexandra. *The Superhuman Life of Gesar of Ling*, Rider, London, 1933.

David-Neel, Alexandra. *With Mystics and Magicians in Tibet*, Penguins, Harmondsworth, 1936.

David-Neel, Alexandra. *The Secret Oral Teachings in Tibetan Buddhist Sects*, Mahabodhi Society, Calcutta, 1950.

Dawa-Samdup, Kazi (ed.). *Srichakra-sambhava Tantra*, Luzac, London, 1919.

De, Sushil Kumar. *Treatment of Love in Sanskrit Literature*, S.K. Das, Calcutta, 1929.

De, Sushil Kumar. *Ancient Indian Erotics and Erotic Literature*, Mukhopadhyay, Calcutta, 1959.

De Mott, Benjamin. *Supergrow*, Gollancz, London, 1970.

Desai, Devaganga. *Erotic Sculpture of India*, Tata McGraw Hill, New Delhi, 1975.

Desmond, Shaw. *Psychic Pitfalls*, Rider, London, 1948.

Devi, Kamala. *The Eastern Way of Love: Tantrik Sex and Erotic Mysticism*, Simon & Schuster, New York, 1977.

Dickhoff, R.E. *Agharta: The Subterranean World*, Dickhoff, New York, 1965.

Diehl, Karl Gustav. *Instrument and Purpose Studies in Rites and Rituals in South India*, Gleerups, Lund, 1956.

Dikshit, S.K. *Mother Goddess*, Eastern Press, Poona, 1943.

Dikshitar, V.R. *The Lalita Cult*, Madras University Press, 1941.

Douglas, Nik. *Tantra Yoga*, Munshiram Manoharlal, New Delhi, 1971.

Douglas, Nik. *Tibetan Tantrik Charms and Amulets*, Dover, New York, 1978.

Douglas, Nik, and Slinger, Penny. *Sexual Secrets: The Alchemy of Ecstasy*, Destiny Books, New York, 1978; Hutchinson, London, 1979.

Douglas, N., and White, M. *The Black Hat Lama of Tibet*, Luzac, London, 1975.

Dubois, The Abbé J.A. *Hindu Manners, Customs and Ceremonies*, Oxford University Press, 1936.

Dutt, Manmatha Nath (ed.). *Mahanirvana Tantram*, 1900; 2nd ed., Chowkhamba Sanskrit Series Office, Varanasi, 1979.

Easwaran, Eknath. *The Mantram Handbook*, Routledge & Kegan Paul, London, 1975.

Ebon, Martin. *The Satan Trap: Dangers of the Occult*, Doubleday, New York, 1976.

Ekvall, Robert. *Religious Observances in Tibet,* Chicago University Press, 1964.

Eliade, Mircea. *Yoga, Immortality and Freedom*, Routledge & Kegan Paul, London; Pantheon, New York, 1958.

Eliade, Mircea. *Shamanism: Archaic Techniques of Ecstasy*, Routledge & Kegan Paul, London, 1964.

Elisifon, E., and Watts, A. *Erotic Spirituality: The Vision of Konarak*, Macmillan, New York, 1971.

Evans-Wentz, Walter Yeeling (ed.). *Tibetan Yoga and Secret Doctrine*, Oxford University Press, 1935.

Evans-Wentz, Walter Yeeling (ed.) *The Tibetan Book of the Great Liberation*, Oxford University Press, 1954.

Evans-Wentz, Walter Yeeling (ed.). *Tibet's Great Yogi Milarepa,* Oxford University Press, 1958.

Fiser, Ivo. *Indian Erotics of the Oldest Period*, Karlova University Press, Prague, 1966.

Foucher, Max-Pol. *The Erotic Sculpture of India*, Allen & Unwin, London; Criterion Books, New York, 1959.

Gait, E.A. *History of Assam*, Government Press, Shillong and Calcutta, 1906.

Gangadhar, V., and Misra, R.K. 'Of Godmen and Porn', *Illustrated Weekly of India*, October 31, 1976.

Gardner, Marshall. *A Journey to the Earth's Interior, or Have the Poles Really Been Discovered?* Aurora, Illinois, 1920.

Garrison, Omar V. *Tantra, the Yoga of Sex*, Julian Press, New York, 1964; Academy Editions, London, 1972.

George, Chris C. (trans.). *The Chandamaharosana Tantra*, American Oriental Society, New Haven, 1974.

Getty, Alice. *The Gods of Northern Buddhism*, Oxford University Press, 1914.

Ghurye, G.S. *Indian Sadhus*, Popular Prakashan, Bombay, 2nd ed., 1964.

Giannini, F. Amadeo. *Worlds Beyond the Poles*, Vantage Press, New York, 1959.

Goldberg, B.Z. *The Sacred Fire: The Story of Sex in Religion*, Jarrolds, London, 1931.

Goswami, Hemchandra (trans. & ed.). *Kamaratna Tantra*, Assam Government Press, Shillong, 1928.

Goswami, Shyam Sundar. *Layayoga*, Routledge & Kegan Paul, London, 1978.

Govinda, Lama Anagarika. *Foundations of Tibetan Mysticism*, Rider, London, 1959; Weiser, New York, 1974.

Govinda, Lama Anagarika. *The Way of the White Clouds*, Hutchinson, London, 1966.

Grant, Kenneth. *Cults of the Shadow*, Muller, London, 1973.

Guenther, Herbert V. *The Life and Teaching of Naropa*, Oxford University Press, 1963.

Guenther, Herbert V. *Yuganaddha. The Tantrik View of Life*, Chowkhamba Sanskrit Series, Varanasi, 1969.

Guenther, Herbert V. *Buddhist Philosophy in Theory and Practice*, Pelican, Harmondsworth, 1972.

Guenther, Herbert V., and Trungpa, Chögyam. *The Dawn of Tantra*, Shambhala, Berkeley and London, 1975.

Gupta, Sanjuka (trans.). *Lakshmi Tantra*, Brill, Leiden, 1972.

Gupta, Shakti M. *Loves of Hindu Gods and Sages*, Allied Publishers, Bombay, 1973.

Haining, Peter. *The Necromancers*, Introduction by Robert Bloch, Hodder & Stoughton, London, 1971.

Hoffmann, Helmut. *The Religions of Tibet*, Allen & Unwin, London, 1961.

Hopkins, Jeffrey (trans.). *Tantra in Tibet: The Great Exposition of Secret Mantra*, Allen & Unwin, London, 1977.

Hopkins, J., and Sugerman, D. *No One Here Gets Out Alive*, Plexus, London, 1980.

Huxley, Aldous. *The Doors of Perception*, Penguin, Harmondsworth, 1959.

Iijima, Kanjitsu. *Buddhist Yoga*, Japan Publications, New York, 1975.

Jacobs, Hans. *Western Psychology and Hindu Sadhana*, Allen & Unwin, London, 1961.

Jacolliot, Louis. *Occult Science in India and Among the Ancients, with an Account of Their Mystic Initiations*, University Books, New York, 1971.

Jaggi, O.P. *Yogic and Tantrik Medicine*, Atma-Ram, Delhi, 1973.

James, E.O. *The Cult of the Mother Goddess*, Thames & Hudson, London; Praeger, New York, 1959.

Janakananda, Swami Saraswati. *Yoga, Tantra and Meditation*, Rider, London, 1978.

Jasper, Tony. *Understanding Pop*, SCM Press, London, 1972.

Jhavery, Mohanlal Bhagwandas. *Comparative and Critical Study of Mantrashastra*, Sarabai Manilal, Ahmedabad, 1944.

Jindal, K.B. *A History of Hindi Literature*, Indian Press, Allahabad, 1955.

Jnanananda, Paramahamsa. *Kaulavali-nirnaya*, with an Introduction by Arthur Avalon, Sanskrit Press Depository, Calcutta, 1928.

Jung, C.G. *Civilization in Transition*, Routledge & Kegan Paul, London, 1964.

Jung, C.G. *Mandala Symbolism*, Princeton University Press, 1972; Routledge & Kegan Paul, London, 1981.

Jyotirmayananda. *Meditate the Tantrik Way*, Allen & Unwin, London, 1973.

Kagal, Ayesha. 'From Guru to God', *Times of India, Sunday Review*, Bombay, June 14, 1981.

Kakati, B.K. *The Mother Goddess Kamakhya*, Lawyers Publications, Gauhati, 1967.

Kale, Arvind and Shanta. *Tantra: The Secret Power of Sex*, Jaico, Bombay, 1976.

Kane, Pandurang Vaman. *Tantras and Dharmasastra*, Bhandarkar Oriental Research Institute, Poona, 1962.

Kaverne, Per. *An Anthology of Buddhist Tantrik Songs*, Columbia University Press, 1977.

Kaviraj, Gopi Nath (ed.). *Goraksha-Siddhanta-Samgraha*, Vidya Vilas Press, Banaras, 1925.

Khanna, Madhu. *Yantra: The Tantrik Symbol of Cosmic Unity*, Thames & Hudson, London, 1979.

King, Francis. *Satan And Swastika: The Occult and the Nazi Party*, Mayflower, London, 1976.

Kingsley, David R. *The Sword and the Flute: Kali and Krsna*, California University Press, 1977.

Kirpekar, Subhash. 'Balyogeshwar vs Bal Bhagwan'. *Illustrated Weekly of India*, May 18, 1975.

Kleen, Tyra. *Mudras: The Ritual Hand-Poses of the Buddha Priests and Shiva Priests of Bali*, Kegan Paul, London, 1924.

Koestler, Arthur. *The Lotus and the Robot*, Hutchinson, London, 1960.

Kooy, K.R. van. *Worship of the Goddess According to the Kalika Purana*, Brill, Leiden, 1972.

Kovoor, Abraham. *Begone Godmen*, Jaico, Bombay, 1975.

Kovoor, Abraham. *Gods, Demons and Spirits*, Jaico, Bombay, 1980.

Kramrisch, Stella. *The Presence of Shiva*, Princeton University Press, 1981.

Krishna, Gopi. *Kundalini: The Evolutionary Energy in Man*, Ramadharand Hopman, New Delhi, 1967; Routledge & Kegan Paul, London, 1971.

Krishna, Gopi. *The Secret of Yoga*, Motilal Banarsidas, Delhi; Harper & Row, New York, 1972.

Krishna, Gopi. *The Biological Basis of Religion and Genius*, Harper & Row, New York, 1973.

Krishna, Gopi. *The Awakening of Kundalini*, Dutton, New York, 1975.

Krishna, Gopi. *Kundalini: Paths to Higher Consciousness*, Orient, Delhi, 1976.

Krishnabai. *Guru's Grace*, Anandashram, Kanhangad, 1964.

Kumar, Pushpendra. *Sakti Cult in Ancient India*, Bhartiya Publishing House, Varanasi, 1974.

Kundalini Research Institute. *Kundalini: Yoga-Sadhana Guidelines*, Kundalini Research Institute, Claremont, California, 1976.

Kuvalayananda, Swami. *Asanas*, Popular Prakashan, Bombay, 1964.

Lal, Kanwar. *The Cult of Desire*, Asia Press, Delhi, 1966.

Lalita. *Choose Your Own Mantra*, Bantam Books, New York, 1978.

La Meri. *The Gesture Language of the Hindu Dance*, Columbia University Press, 1941.

Lauf, Detlef Ingo. *Secret Doctrines of the Tibetan Books of the Dead*, Shambhala, Berkeley and London, 1977.

Laufer, Berthold. *Use of Human Skulls and Bones in Tibet*, Museum of Natural History, Chicago, 1923.

Laurent, E., and Nagour, P. *Magica Sexualis: Black Arts and Secret Sciences*, Falstaff Press, New York, 1934.

Leadbeater, C.W. *The Chakras*, Theosophical Publishing House, London; Wheaton, Illinois; Adyar, Madras, 1972.

Leeson, Francis. *Kama Shilpa*, Taraporevala, Bombay, 1962.

Lessing, F.D., and Wayman, Alex. *Fundamentals of the Buddhist Tantras*, Mouton, The Hague, 1968.

LeShan, Lawrence. *How to Meditate*, Wildwood House, London, 1978.

Lipton, Lawrence. *The Holy Barbarians*, W.H. Allen, London, 1960.

Lorenzen, D.N. *The Kapalikas and Kalamukhas*, Thomson Press, New Delhi, 1972.

Luk, Charles (Lu K'uan Yü). *Taoist Yoga: Alchemy and Immortality*, Rider, London, 1970.

Maclellan, Alec. *The Lost World of Agharti*, Souvenir Press, London, 1982.

Macunn, Sir George. *The Religious and Hidden Cults of India*, London, n.d.

Majumdar, R.C. (ed.). *The Age of Imperial Unity*, Bharatiya Vidya Bhavan, Bombay, 1960.

Mallik, Kalyani. *Siddha-Siddhanta-paddati, and Other Works of Natha Yogis*, Indian Press, Poona, 1954.

Maraini, Fosco. *Secret Tibet*, Hutchinson, London, 1952; Grove Press, New York, 1960.

Marshall, Anne. *Hunting the Guru in India*, Gollancz, London, 1963.

156 TANTRISM

Matson, Katinka. *The Encyclopedia of Reality*, Paladin, London, 1979.

Mehta, Gita. *Karma Cola*, Simon & Schuster, New York, 1979; Fontana, London, 1981.

Menen, Aubrey. *The New Mystics*, Thames & Hudson, London, 1974.

Metzner, Ralph. *Maps of Consciousness: I Ching, Tantra, Tarot, Alchemy, Astrology, Actualism*, Macmillan, New York, 1971.

Meyer, Johann Jakob. *Sexual Life in Ancient India*, 2 vols., Dutton, New York, 1930; Routledge & Kegan Paul, London, 1953.

Miles, A. *Land of the Lingam*, Hurst & Blackett, London, 1933.

Mishra, R.S. *Yoga Sutras*, Doubleday, New York, 1973.

Mishra, R.S. *Fundamentals of Yoga*, Anchor, New York, 1974.

Moffett, Robert K. *Tantric Sex*, Berkeley Publishing Corporation, New York, 1974.

Mookerjee, Ajit. *Tantra Asana: A Way to Self Realization*, Ravi Kumar, Basel and New Delhi, 1971.

Mookerjee, Ajit. *Tantra Art: Its Philosophy and Physics*, Ravi Kumar, Basel and New Delhi, 1972.

Mookerjee, Ajit, and Anand, Mulk Raj. *Tantra Magic*, Arnold-Heinemann, New Delhi, 1977.

Mookerjee, Ajit, and Khanna, Madhu. *The Tantrik Way: Art, Science, Ritual*, Thames & Hudson, London; New York Graphic, New York, 1977.

Mookerji, R.K. *Rasa-jala-nidhi: or Ocean of Indian Chemistry and Alchemy*, 5 vols., Calcutta University Press, 1926-38.

Morrison, Blake. 'The Sound of the Sixties', *Times Literary Supplement*, London, May 15, 1981.

Motoyama, Hiroshi. *Chakra: Nadi of Yoga, and Meridian Points of Acupuncture*, Institute of Religious Psychology, Tokyo, 1972.

Murphet, Howard. *Sai Baba: Man of Miracles*, Muller, London, 1971.

Muses, C.A. *Esoteric Teachings of Tibetan Tantra*, Aurora Press, Lausanne, 1961.

Nagaswamy, R. *Tantrik Cult in South India*, Agam Prakasham, Delhi, 1980.

Narasimhaiah, Dr H. 'Sathya Sai Baba – God or Fraud? *Illustrated Weekly of India*, October 31, 1976.

Narayanananda, Swami. *The Primal Power in Man: The Kundalini Shakti*, N.K. Prasad, Rishikesh; Yoga Trust and Ashram, Gylling, Denmark, 1950.

Narayanananda, Swami. *The Secrets of Prana*, N.K. Prasad, Rishikesh, 1959.

Narayanananda, Swami. *The Mysteries of Man, Mind, and Mind Functions*, N.K. Prasad, Rishikesh, 1965.

Nebesky-Wojkowitz, René de. *Oracles and Demons of Tibet*, Oxford University Press, 1956.

Needleman, Jacob. *The New Religions*, Allen Lane, London; Doubleday, New York, 1970.

Neelakontan, V.T., and Ramaiah, S.A.A. *Death of Death*, S.A.A. Ramaiah, Madras, 1965.

Neumann, Erich. *The Great Mother: An Analysis of the Archetype*, Routledge & Kegan Paul, London, 1955; Princeton University Press, 1972.

Nikhilananda, Swami. *Hinduism: Its Meaning for the Liberation of the Spirit*, Allen & Unwin, London, 1959.

Nivedita, Sister. *Kali the Mother*, Advaita Ashram, Mayavati, 1953.

Norman, Philip. *Shout! The True Story of the Beatles*, Elm Tree Books, London, 1981.

O'Flaherty, Wendy. *Asceticism and Eroticism in the Mythology of Shiva*, Oxford University Press, 1973.

Olson, Eleanor. *Tantrik Buddhist Art*, China Institute in America, New York, 1974.

Oman, J.C. *The Mystics, Ascetics and Saints of India*, Fisher Unwin, London, 1905.

Oman, J.C. *Cults, Customs and Superstitions of India*, Fisher Unwin, London, 1908.

Ossendowski, Ferdinand. *Beasts, Men and Gods*, Edward Arnold, London, 1923.

Pallis, Marco. *Peaks and Lamas*, Cassell, London, 1939.

Pandey, Kanti Chandra. *Abhinavagupta: An Historical and Philosophical Study*, Chowkhamba Sanskrit Series, Varanasi, 1963.

Pandit, M.P. *Lights on the Tantra*, Ganesh, Madras, 1957.

Pandit, M.P. *Kundalini Yoga*, Ganesh, Madras, 1978.

Pandit, M.P. *Studies in the Tantra and the Veda*, Ganesh, Madras, 1964.

Pandit, M.P. *Sri Aurobindo on the Tantra*, Aurobindo Ashram, Pondicherry, 1967.

Pandit, M.P. *Gems from the Tantras: Series I and II*, Ganesh, Madras, 1969, 1970.

Pandit, M.P. *Kularnava Tantra*, Ganesh, Madras, 1973.

Parab, B.A. *The Miraculous and Mysterious in Vedic Literature*, Parab, Bombay, 1952.

Parrinder, Geoffrey. *Mysticism in the World's Religions*, Sheldon Press, London, 1976.

Patanjali. *Yoga-Sutra*, translated by Bengali Baba, Bhargawa, Poona, 1949.

Pathak, V.S. *History of Saiva Cults in Northern India*, Ram Naresh Varma, Varanasi, 1960.

Pauwels, Louis, and Bergier, Jacques. *The Dawn of Magic*, Gibbs & Phillips, London, 1963.

Pawar, P. 'Did Tantriks Kill Nehru?' *Mirror*, Bombay, April 1981.

Payne, Ernest A. *The Saktas*, YMCA Publishing House, Calcutta, 1933.

Pinkham, Mildred. *Women in the Sacred Scriptures of Hinduism*, Allen & Unwin, London, 1943.

Pott, P.H. *Yoga and Yantra*, Martinus Nijhoff, The Hague, 1966.

Prabhavananda, Swami. *Yoga and Mysticism*, Vedanta Press, Hollywood, 1972.

Prakash, Vidya. *Khajuraho*, Taraporevala, Bombay, 1967.

Prem, Sri Krishna. *The Yoga of the Bhagavad Gita*, Penguin, Baltimore, 1973.

Radha, Swami Sivananda. *Kundalini Yoga for the West,* Shambhala, London, 1981.

Rai, A.K. *Kundalini the Goddess*, Central Press, Calcutta, 1908.

Rajneesh, Bhagwan Shree. *The Book of the Secrets: Discourses on Vigyana Bhairava Tantra*, Thames & Hudson, London, 1976.

Rajneesh, Bhagwan Shree. *Meditation: The Art of Ecstasy*, Harper & Row, New York, 1977.

Rajneesh, Bhagwan Shree. *The Tantra Vision*, Rajneesh Foundation, Poona, 2 vols., 1979.

Ramacharaka, Yogi. *The Hindu-Yogi Science of Breath*, Yogi Publishing Co., Chicago, 1925.

Ramacharaka, Yogi. *Yogi Philosophy and Oriental Occultism*, Yogi Publishing Co., Chicago, 1931.

Rambach, Pierre. *The Secret Message of Tantrik Buddhism*, Rizzoli, New York, 1978.

Rao, S.K. Ramachandra. *Tibetan Tantrik Tradition*, Arnold-Heinemann, New Delhi, 1977.

Ravenscroft, Trevor. *The Spear of Destiny*, Spearman, London, 1972; Bantam Books, New York, 1974.

Rawson, Philip. *Tantra: The Indian Cult of Ecstasy*, Thames & Hudson, London; Avon Books, New York, 1973.

Rawson, Philip. *The Art of Tantra*, New York Graphic Society, Greenwich, Connecticut; Thames and Hudson, London, 1974.

Rawson, Philip. *Erotic Art of India*, Thames & Hudson, London, 1978.

Ray, T.N. (ed.). *Kokokam and Rati Rahasyam*, Medical Book Co., Calcutta, 1960.

Rele, Vasant G. *The Mysterious Kundalini*, Taraporevala, Bombay, 1927.

Rele, Vasant G. *Yogic Asanas*, Taraporevala, Bombay, 1960.

Renan, Sheldon. *The Underground Film*, Dutton, New York; Studio Vista, London, 1968.

Rendel, Peter. *Introduction to Chakras*, Aquarian Press, London, 1974.

Rieker, Hans Ulrich. *The Yoga of Light: Hatha Yoga Pradipika*, Dawn House Press, Los Angeles; Allen & Unwin, London, 1974.

Riepe, D. *The Naturalistic Tradition in Indian Thought*, Washington University Press, Seattle, 1961.

Rivière, J. Marquès. *Tantrik Yoga: Hindu and Tibetan*, Aquarian Press, London; Weiser, New York, 1973.

Robbins, Jhan, and Fisher, David. *Tranquility Without Pills: All About Transcendental Meditation*, Souvenir Press, London, 1973.

Roerich, George N. *Trails to Innermost Asia*, Yale University Press, 1931.

Roerich, George N. (trans.). *The Blue Annals (History of the Spread of Buddhism in Tibet)*, 2 vols., Calcutta University Press, 1949, 1953.

Roerich, Nicholas. *Heart of Asia*, Jarrolds, London, 1929.

Roerich, Nicholas. *Altai-Himalaya*, Jarrolds, London, 1930.

Roerich, Nicholas. *Himalayas: Abode of Light*, David Marlowe, London, 1947.

Samdup, Lama Kazi Dawa. *Chakrasambhara Tantra*, Luzac, London, 1910.

Sana, Kshanika. *Buddhism and Buddhist Literature in Central Asia*, Mukhopadhyay, Calcutta, 1970.

Sanella, Lee. *Kundalini: Psychosis or Transcendence*, Human Science Press, New York, 1976.

Sankarananda, Swami. *Is Siva-Lingam a Phallus?* Nilmoni Maharaj, Calcutta, 1957.

Saraswati, Swami Janakananda. *Yoga, Tantra and Meditation in Everyday Life*, Rider, London, 1978.

Saraswati, Swami Pratyagatmananda. *The Metaphysics of Physics: The Background of Modern Cosmological Conception in Vedic and Tantrik Symbolism*, Ganesh, Madras, 1964.

Saraswati, Swami Pratyagatmananda. *Japasutram: A Study in Tantra Shastra*, Ganesh, Madras, 1971.

Saraswati, Swami Pratyagatmananda. *Sadhana for Self-Realization: Mantras, Yantras, and Tantras*, Ganesh, Madras, 1973.

Saraydarian, Torkom. *The Legend of Shamballa*, Aquarian Educational Group, San Fransisco, 1976.

Sarcar, S.C. *Some Aspects of the Earliest Social History of India*, Oxford University Press, 1928.

Sastry, K. *The Veda and the Tantras*, Ganesh, Madras, 1951.

Saunders, E. Dale. *Mudra*, Routledge & Kegan Paul, London, 1960.

Schmidt, Toni. *The Eighty-Five Siddhas*, Schmidt, Stockholm, 1958.

Schoterman, J.A. *The Yonitantra*, Manohar Publications, New Delhi, 1980.

Sen, R. *Ascetic Enjoyment: Its Background in Philosophy and Medicine*, Calcutta University Press, 1966.

Sharma, Y.S. *Sri Kundalini*, Sakthi Serpent Power, Bangalore, 1971.

Sharpe, Elizabeth. *The Philosophy of Yoga*, Luzac, London, 1933.

Sharpe, Elizabeth. *The Secrets of the Kaula Circle*, London, 1936.

Shastri, H.P. (ed.). *Advayavajra-Samgraha: A collection of the Aphorisms of Advayavajra, a Famous Buddhist Tantrik Teacher*, Gaekwad Oriental Series, Baroda, 1927.

Shastri, Mukund Ram (ed.). *The Tantrasara of Abhinava Gupta*, Nirnaya Sagar Press, Bombay, 1918.

Shekhar, Chandra. *Passage to Divinity*, Anandashram Publishing Co., Anandashram, 1955.

Shivapadmasundaram, S. *The Shaiva School of Hinduism*, Madras University Press, 1934.

Sierksma, F. *Tibet's Terrifying Deities: Sex and Aggression in Religious Acculturation,* Mouton, The Hague; Tuttle, Rutland, Vermont, 1966.

Singh, Khushwant. 'Hot Line to God', *Illustrated Weekly of India,* Bombay, August 1, 1976.

Singh, Lalan Prasad. *Tantra: Its Mystic and Scientific Basis,* Motilal Banarsidas, Delhi, 1977.

Singh, Mohan. *Gorakhnath and Medieval Hindu Mysticism,* Panjab Printers, Lahore, 1937.

Sinh, Pancham (trans.). *Hatha Yoga Pradipika,* 2nd ed., Panini Office, Allahabad, 1932.

Sinha, J. *Sakta Monism: The Cult of Shakti,* Calcutta University Press, 1966.

Sinistrari, L.M. *Demonality or Incubi and Succubi,* edited by Montague Summers, Fortune Press, London, 1927.

Sircar, D.C. *The Shakti Cult and Tara,* Calcutta University Press, 1967.

Sircar, D.C. *The Sakta Pithas,* 2nd rev. ed., Orient, New Delhi, 1973.

Sircar, M.N. *Hindu Mysticism According to the Upanishads,* Orient, New Delhi, 1973.

Sitney, P. Adams. *Visionary Film,* Oxford University Press, New York, 1974.

Sivananda, Swami. *Kundalini Yoga,* Yogi-Vedanta Forest Academy, Sivanandanagar, 1968.

Snehi, B.K., and Saxena, Rajeev. 'The Guru, Goenka and the Government', *Probe,* Allahabad, March 1981.

Snellgrove, David L. (ed.). *The Hevajra Tantra,* 2 vols., Oxford University Press, 1959.

Snellgrove, David L. (ed.). *The Nine Ways of Bon,* Oxford University Press, 1967; Routledge & Kegan Paul, London, 1981.

Spence, Lewis. *The Occult Causes of the Present War,* Rider, London, 1940.

Strachey, Ray C. *Religious Fanaticism,* Faber, London, 1928.

Swami, Shree Purohit (ed.). *Patanjali's Aphorisms of Yoga,* Faber, London, 1973.

Swarup, B. *Konarak: The Black Pagoda,* Signet Press, Calcutta, 1910.

Tamhankar, Arun. 'Tantra', *Mirror,* Bombay, April, 1981.

Tattuabhushan, Hemachandra (trans.). *Kamaratna Tantra*, Steam Press, Shillong, 1928.

Taylor, Capt. Meadows. *Confessions of a Thug*, Bentley, London, 1839.

Thinley, Karma. *The History of the Sixteen Karmapas of Tibet,* Routledge & Kegan Paul, London, 1981.

Thirleby, A. *Tantra: The Key to Sexual Power and Pleasure*, Dell Books, New York, 1978.

Thomas, P. *Kama-Kala: The Hindu Ritual of Love*, Taraporevala, Bombay, 1963.

Thompson, E.J., and Spencer, A.M. (eds. and trans.). *Bengali Religious Lyrics*, Oxford University Press, 1923.

Tomas, Andrew. *Shambhala: Oasis of Light*, Sphere Books, London, 1977.

Trungpa, Chogyam. *Mudra*, Shambhala, Berkeley; Routledge & Kegan Paul, London, 1972.

Trungpa, Chogyam. *Visual Dharma: The Buddhist Art of Tibet*, Shambhala, Berkeley, 1975.

Tsuda, Shinichi. *The Samvarodaya Tantra*, Kokuseido Press, Tokyo, 1974.

Tucci, Gieseppe. *Tibetan Painted Scrolls*, 3 vols., State Library, Rome, 1949.

Tucci, Giuseppe. *The Theory and Practice of the Mandala*, Rider, London, 1961; Weiser, New York, 1970.

Tucci, Giuseppe. *Rati Lila: An Interpretation of the Tantrik Imagery of the Temples of Nepal*, Nagel, Geneva, 1969.

Tucci, Giuseppe. *The Religions of Tibet*, Routledge & Kegan Paul, London, 1980.

Upadhya, B.C. *Women in Rigveda*, 2nd ed., Nand Kishore, Banaras, 1941.

Upadhyaya, S.C. (trans.). *Kama Sutra: Illustrated Edition, Taraporevala, Bombay, 1963.*

Vasu, Sris Chandra (trans.). *Gheranda Samhita*, Tatva-Vivechaka Press, Bombay, 1895.

Vidyarnava, Srisa Chandra (trans.). *Siva Samhita*, 2nd ed., Panini Office, Allahabad, 1923.

Vivekananda, Swami. *The Yogas and Other Works*, Ramakrishna and Vivekananda Center, New York, 1953.

Vliet, C.J. van. *The Coiled Serpent*, Navajivan Press, Ahmedabad, 1963.

Vogel, J.P. *Indian Serpent Lore*, Arthur Probsthain, London, 1926.

Volin, Michael, and Phetan, Nancy. *Sex and Yoga*, Pelham Books, London, 1967.

Waddell, L. Austin. *The Buddhism of Tibet, or Lamaism*, W.H. Allen, London, 1895; Dover, New York, 1972.

Waite, A.E. *Book of Black Magic and Pacts*, Rider, London, 1898.

Wake, S. Staniland. *Serpent Worship and Other Essays*, Redway, London, 1888.

Walker, Benjamin. *Hindu World*, 2 vols., Allen & Unwin, London; Praeger, New York, 1968.

Walker, Benjamin. *Sex and the Supernatural*, Macdonald, London; Harper & Row, New York, 1973.

Walker, Benjamin. *Encyclopedia of Esoteric Man*, Routledge & Kegan Paul, London; Stein & Day, New York, 1977.

Warder, A.K. *Indian Buddhism*, Motilal Banarsidas, Delhi, 1970.

Watts, Allan, and Eliot, Elisofon. *Erotic Spirituality: The Vision of Konarak*, Collier, New York, 1971.

Wayman, Alex. *The Buddhist Tantras: Light on Indo-Tibetan Esotericism*, Routledge & Kegan Paul, London, 1973.

Wayman, Alex. *Yoga of the Guhyasamaja Tantra: The Arcane Lore of Forty Verses*, Motilal Banarsidas, Delhi, 1977.

Webb, James. *The Occult Establishment*, Open Court, La Salle, Illinois 1976.

Webb, James. *The Harmonious Circle*, Thames & Hudson, London, 1980.

Webb, Peter. *The Erotic Arts*, Secker & Warburg, London, 1975.

Welch, Holmes. *The Parting of the Way: Lao Tzu and the Taoist Movement*, Methuen, London, 1957.

Weldon, John. *The Transcendental Explosion*, Harvest House, Irvine, 1976.

Weldon, John, and Wilson, Clifford. *Occult Shock and Psychic Forces*, Master Books, San Diego, California, 1980.

Werner, E.T.C. *A Dictionary of Chinese Mythology*, Julian Press, New York, 1961.

Wessels, M. *Early Jesuit Travellers in Central Asia*, Mouton, The Hague, 1924.

White, John (ed.). *What is Meditation?* Anchor, New York, 1974.

White, John (ed.). *Everything You Always Wanted to Know About TM*, Anchor, New York, 1974.

White, John (ed.). *Kundalini: Catastrophe or Creative Consciousness*, Human Dimensions Institute, New York, 1976.

White, John (ed.). *Kundalini: Evolution and Enlightenment*, Doubleday, New York, 1979.

Wintle, Justin (ed.). *Makers of Modern Culture*, Routledge & Kegan Paul, London, 1981.

Wood, Ernest. *The Occult Training of the Hindus*, Rider, London, 1931.

Wood, Ernest. *Great Systems of Yoga*, Rider, London, 1954.

Wood, Ernest. *Yoga*, Penguin, Harmondsworth, 1959.

Woodroffe, Sir John (Arthur Avalon). *Kalivilasa Tantra*, Luzac, London, 1917.

Woodroffe, Sir John. *Tantaraja Tantra*, Ganesh, Madras, 1951; Vedanta Press, Hollywood, 1954.

Woodroffe, Sir John. *Hymn to Kali. Translation and Commentary of Karpuradistotram*, Ganesh, Madras, 1952.

Woodroffe, Sir John. *Hymns to the Goddess*, Ganesh, Madras, 1953.

Woodroffe, Sir John. *The Greatness of Shiva*, Vedanta Press, Hollywood, 1953.

Woodroffe, Sir John. *Varnamala, or The Garland of Letters: Studies in Mantra-sastra*, Ganesh, Madras, 1954.

Woodroffe, Sir John. *Kamakala-vilasa*, Ganesh, Madras, 1955.

Woodroffe, Sir John. *Shakti and Shakta*, Ganesh, Madras, 1956.

Woodroffe, Sir John. *Kulachudamani Nigama*, 2nd ed., Vedanta Press, Hollywood, 1956.

Woodroffe, Sir John. *Introduction to Tantra Sastra: A Key to Tantrik Literature*, 3rd ed., Ganesh, Madras, 1957.

Woodroffe, Sir John. *The Serpent Power: Translation and Commentary on Two Tantrik Texts on the Kundalini*, 6th ed., Ganesh, Madras, 1958.

Woodroffe, Sir John. *Principles of Tantra: Translation and Commentary of a 19th Century Bengali Treatise, Tantra-tattva*, 2nd ed., Ganesh, Madras, 1959.

Woodroffe, Sir John. *Kularnava Tantra*, Ganesh, Madras, 1965.

Woodroffe, Sir John. *The World as Power*, Ganesh, Madras, 1966.

Woodroffe, Sir John. *Tantra of the Great Liberation (Mahanirvana Tantra)*, Dover, New York, 1972.

Woodroffe, Sir John, and Sastri, Pandit Sitaram (eds.). *Kaula and Other Upanishads*, Luzac, London, 1922.

Woods, James Hughton (trans.). *Yoga-system of Patanjali*, Motilal Banarsidas, Delhi, 1966.

Yogi, Maharishi Mahesh. *Transcendental Meditation*, Signet, New York, 1968.

Yogi, Maharishi Mahesh. *Meditations of Maharishi Mahesh Yogi*, Bantam, New York, 1973.

Yogi, Maharishi Mahesh. *Commentary on the Bhagavad Gita*, Penguin, Baltimore, 1974.

Zaehner, R. C. *Drugs, Mysticism and Make-Believe*, Collins, London, 1972.

INDEX

scatology, 32, 33, 83
Schoterman, J. A., 59, 63, 72
scientology, 111
Scott, Michael, 110
Sebottendorff, Rudolf von, 114
secrecy, 15
sects, 99
Sellon, Edward, 105
semen, 10, 39, 40, 41, 45, 51, 52, 93
Sena, 101
sensitivity training, 139
sex in religion, 32, 47, 48, 58
shabda, 22
Shaivites, 100
Shakta, 68, 80, 100
Shakti, 10, 43, 58, 59, 65, 68, 84
Shakti-sangama Tantra, 98
shamanism, 87
Shambhala, 88, 89, 90, 94, 99, 114
Shani, 100
Sharpe, E., 97
Shastri, D. R., 99
Shatapata Brahmana, 60
shava, 82
shava-asana, 81
Shava-vada, 82, 84, 100
Shenrab, 91, 95
Shepala, 100
shiatzu, 139
Shingon, 58, 94
shirsha-asana (see headstand)
Shiva, 10, 11, 43, 50, 54, 56, 59-61, 63, 68, 82, 84, 100
Shiva Purana, 61
shloka, 22, 143
shri-yantra, 20
shunya, 63
Shveta-dvipa, 88
Shvetaketu, 71
Siddha, 46, 56, 91, 98, 100

siddha-asana, 122
siddhi, 14, 46, 56, 130
Sierksma, F., 33, 50, 63, 81, 85, 96, 127
Sita, 63
Sitney, P.A., 119
Smith, Harry, 119
Smith, Jack, 119
Smith, W. T., 111
Snehi, B. K., and Saxena, R., 137
Snellgrove, David, 121
Solomon, 110
soma, 56
Somapura, 101
Sophia, 69
sound, 22
Spare, A. O., 112
spermepotation, 39
spine, 36
spinning, 9
squaring the circle, 21
Srong-tsan-gam-po, 16
SS (Schutzstaffe), 113
Steiner, Rudolf, 109, 110, 112
Stone, Randolph, 139
Strabo, 56
Strachey, R.C., 106
stri-puja, 50, 69
stri-rajya, 90
Subterra, 89
subtle congress (see *congressus subtilis*)
subud, 139
Subuh, Muhammad, 139
succubus, 74
Sufi, 41, 129, 139
Sukhavati, 62
sulphur, 55
Sumeria, 88
Sumeru, 87
Surya, 100
sushumna, 45

Vishnu, 15, 57, 59, 82
vishuddha, 42
Vishvasara Tantra, 36
Vivekananda, Swami, 129, 132
vulva, 62
Vyali, 57

Waley, Arthur, 52
Walker, Benjamin, 40, 53, 54, 61
walking on water, 130, 131, 132
Warhol, Andy, 119
weaving, 9
Webb, P., 118, 119
White, John, 138
wife, 70
Wilson, C., and Weldon, J., 114, 126, 137, 138
wine, 32, 65, 68
woman, 47, 50, 68, 70

Wood, Ernest, 125
Woodroffe, Sir John, 61, 74, 105, 121

xenophrenia, 21, 24, 53, 67, 117

yab-yum, 85, 90, 94
Yajnavalkya, 70
yang, 92, 94
yantra, 20
yidam, 27
yin, 40, 92
yie men, 93
yoga, 35, 37, 121
yoni (see vulva)
yoni puja, 63
Yoni Tantra, 59, 63, 69, 82
Yuga, 12

Zen, 93, 94
Zok-chen-pa, 97
Zoroastrianism, 89